Meet Me in Munich

Author

Moses Wolff, born in 1969 in Munich, is an actor, comedian, author, and Oktoberfest professional. He writes regularly for the satire magazine *Titanic*. He loves Oktoberfest more than anything else and lives in Isarvorstadt, Munich.

Photographer

Volker Derlath, also from Munich, is an art photographer. He is a winner of the Schwabing Art Prize and is known for his photo column in the *Süddeutsche Zeitung*, "Die andere Seite" ("The Other Side").

Meet Me in Munich

A Beer Lover's Guide to Oktoberfest

MOSES WOLFF

photographs by **VOLKER DERLATH**

translated by Tobi Haberstroh

SKYHORSE PUBLISHING

Originally published in Germany under the title *Ozapft is! Das Wiesn-Handbuch*, by Moses Wolff

Copyright © 2012, 2013 by Wilhelm Goldmann Verlag, a division of Verlagsgruppe Random House GmbH, München, Germany
Translation copyright © 2013 by Skyhorse Publishing, Inc.
Photos © Volker Derlath
Illustrations © Moses Wolff

Skyhorse Publishing books may be purchased in bulk at special discounts for sales promotion, corporate gifts, fund-raising, or educational purposes. Special editions can also be created to specifications. For details, contact the Special Sales Department, Skyhorse Publishing, 307 West 36th Street, 11th Floor, New York, NY 10018 or info@skyhorsepublishing.com.

Skyhorse® and Skyhorse Publishing® are registered trademarks of Skyhorse Publishing, Inc.®, a Delaware corporation.

Visit our website at www.skyhorsepublishing.com.

10 9 8 7 6 5 4 3 2 1

Library of Congress Cataloging-in-Publication Data is available on file.

ISBN: 978-1-62636-258-1

Printed in China

For Bazi

No mischief, please!

Contents

It Begins with the Build

Every year in the middle of July, about two months before the beginning of the most famous folk festival in the world, the first semitrailers arrive at the Theresienwiese—the grounds where Oktoberfest is held each year—in Munich. Busy craftsmen and master tent builders search for the spot assigned to them by the Bavarian capital's department of tourism. Slowly but surely they raise giant beer tents and colorful carnival rides on the large paved field in the middle of Munich. Builders work up in the windy heights of roller coasters or move the load-bearing pieces of a beer tent into position.

Beer drinkers of the world, unite!

Some people are already raising their mugs during the build.

Most people have no idea how difficult it is to build a tent like that. I'm fascinated every time I see it. Everything begins with the girders—those huge, weight-bearing pieces that form the skeleton of each festival hall. Bit by bit the aisles, ceiling, and inner workings of the tent appear. Everything is built in quick succession: balcony rigs, floorboards, planks, beams, electronics. Finally, the decorations are put up, nailed, and secured. All around you hear banging and drilling, screwing and hammering, rattling and humming. But there's something for your eyes and nose, too: it smells like resin, and you can see plaques, busts, statues, wreaths, decorative vats, puppets, and lighting equipment lying everywhere.

The entire Wiesn comes to life. Inside, carpenters hammer the beams of the tents in place; outside, TÜV (*Technischer Überwachungsverein*—Technical Inspection Association) workers check the rides for safety. Heavy trucks and utility vans are parked all around. Hundreds of people are at work, stress-free but highly productive. Everyone is buzzing around chaotically.

To this day, I go every year with my mother at the beginning of the build on the Theresienwiese. We love the noise, the atmosphere, the smell, and the luxury to be able to live in a city like this and experience such a wonderful folk festival coming to life in the flesh. For me as a self-avowed Oktoberfest fan, all the fun begins here, during the build.

Oktoberfest is sort of like a roller coaster that you get on in the middle of July with butterflies in your stomach. The roller coaster climbs higher each day, then suddenly

plunges into two turbulent, thrilling weeks before end-
ing in early October with a highly satisfying finale. Then
you cheerfully await the next round. I always take great
joy in the beginning of this ride.

I can still remember attending the build for the first
time with my school friends when I was about nine
years old. We took the S-Bahn from Pasing to Hackerbrücke and walked over to the Theresienwiese. Honestly, we had expected to arrive at a sort of folk festival
ghost town, since it was still weeks until the tapping—
that wonderful ceremony that marks the official beginning of Oktoberfest with a clean mallet strike. We boys
were quite surprised when we arrived and, instead of a
complete but dead fairground, found half-finished tent
structures, diligent handymen, showmen running this
way and that, and countless busily humming trucks
and trailers. An older Munich local who was sitting
on a bench on the edge of the Theresienwiese noticed
our bewilderment. As I recall, he spoke in a thick
Bavarian accent and said, somewhat disapprovingly,
"You could all put yourselves to good use over there."
A moment later he had an epiphany: "Why don't these
people let this rubbish just stay here the whole year?
Then they wouldn't have to go through all this trouble every year." At the time I didn't have an answer for
that quite legitimate question, but today I would say:
"Because then there wouldn't be a build, and that's a big
part of the tradition. That's obvious." Not to mention

that many other events happen on the Theresienwiese during the rest of the year.

Excitement for the greatest event of the year grows in the hearts of every true Munich citizen as soon as the Oktoberfest build begins. It means there's really just a few weeks until Oktoberfest is kicked off with the cry of *"Ozapft is!"*—"It's tapped!"

Since physical needs must also be taken care of during a build like this, there are a few "tent canteens," where workers can buy good food and drink for a reasonable price. After onlookers and wanderers began showing up during the build, it was tolerated but not officially allowed for outsiders to enjoy the canteens. It never got out of hand and never became a problem,

For those who just can't wait: the Oktoberfest canteen.

The Word "Oktoberfest"
About 90 percent of the world's population knows the word "Oktoberfest." That makes it the most famous German word.

but nevertheless at some point a worker ID became a requirement for enjoying beer and chicken in the canteen under the summer sun. However, if one simply sits down and doesn't eat anything, no one says anything. Or so I'm told.

History of the Munich Oktoberfest

The Founding of Munich

In the middle of the eighth century, as the story goes, two monks from the Schäftlarn Cloister made their way farther north in their search for a peaceful, beautiful place to find reflection and refreshment. On the way, they rested on a small hill ringed with trees. After eating the food they had brought, they were both thirsty, and they drank the delicious, crystal-clear water from a rushing river nearby.

"Oh, what good it would do me if this water were even sweeter tasting," cried one monk, and the other surely agreed immediately.

Perhaps they said a prayer that one day a refreshing drink—similar to the already well-known beer—would be served here, which people could quaff by day or night. In any case, in the end they decided to build a wooden church right on that spot and named it in the traditional manner, after St. Petrus. Both spoke quite sophisticated German and traditional Celtic, but, as good monks, also a bit of Latin, and so they named that long-awaited drink "Salvator" ("Healer of the World"), the hill "Petersbergl,"

Empty already!

and the water "ys ura" ("quickly flowing water"). They lived in humility and gratitude until the end of their days.

Four hundred years later, Henry the Lion, Duke of Bavaria and Saxony, built a grand bridge to connect one bank of the river to the other (in the meantime, the river's name had evolved from "ys ura" to the easier to pronounce "Isar"). By then there was a cloister church on that spot. The Duke loved the area and the little islands at the base of the bridge. But he loved commerce even more. So, as a precautionary measure, he left the Oberföhringer Bridge in the more northern diocese of Freising in rubble. The Oberföhringer Bridge had previously been economically indispensible, but with his own bridge (now the only one for miles), Henry could better control horse and cart traffic and boost the state treasury with a hefty toll.

So that everything was in order, he went to Augsburg and applied for the right to levy tolls and fees, which Frederick I Barbarossa gladly granted him. Henry the Lion looked forward to the day far in the future when that spot would become the "northernmost Italian city."

The earliest documentation of the name of Italy's northernmost city is in the "Augsburger Schied," a document written by Frederick I on July 14, 1158. Mentioned in this document is "forum apud . . . Munichen," meaning a market near "Munichen." "Munich" is not only the English word for the city, but also an Old High German word which later became "Münich, Münech, Münch." Then it became "Mönch," the German word for monk. Thus the city name "München" came from monks, probably the very ones who lived on Petersbergl.

The Development of Oktoberfest

The original October folk festival, still popular all over Bavaria, was for the purpose of consuming all of the leftover Märzen beer before the beginning of the new brewing season. The brewing season traditionally begins with the purchase of the ingredients in the fall and ends in the spring, because, among other reasons, there was a much higher prevalence of brewery fires in the "hot" summer months. Märzen beer is a bottom-fermented lager. It is characterized by being a little bit stronger than a regular Helles or pale lager in every sense: the taste and the color as well as the alcohol content are all a bit stronger. Helles is to Märzen as regular gasoline is to premium.

However, the world-renowned Munich Oktoberfest has an entirely different source: a wedding.

On October 12, 1810, Crown Prince Ludwig (the future Ludwig I of Bavaria) married Princess Therese Charlotte Luise von Saxony-Hildburghausen, having snatched her right out from under Napoleon's nose. Five days after the marriage there was a horse race among the festivities, attended by many high-ranking figures. The race was

Some tie a red ribbon around their finger, but others find more interesting ways to remember things.

held on a meadow in front of the gates of Munich, and to honor the young bride, it was named after her, Theresienwiese, or "Therese's Meadow."

On the good advice of an advisor, the Crown Prince decided to hold a festival each year in October—but in the style of the ancient Olympic Games. Ludwig followed the trends of Classicism and Neohumanism; he was a passionate devotee of Greek antiquity, and so he was immediately taken with the idea of presenting an Oktoberfest Olympics. He loved the thought of transforming Munich into "Athens on the Isar."

Not much at Oktoberfest is still reminiscent of the original "Olympian" plan—unless you stand right in front of the statue of Bavaria and look toward the *Ruhmeshalle* (literally *hall of fame*). If you do that, you should also take a moment to close your eyes and imagine yourself at the foot of the Bavaria statue in the middle of the nineteenth century (maybe even during a beautiful sunset). The Theresienwiese is not a paved space in the middle of the hustle and bustle, but rather a real meadow just outside the city, with nothing but nature and the distant horizon in sight. Only this huge statue rises against the sky in front of this classical temple. Everyone should perform this experiment at least once during a visit to Oktoberfest. For Ludwig I's sake.

The architect Leo von Klenze only began planning the Ruhmeshalle a good twenty years after the first Oktoberfest. A short while later, the sculptor Ludwig Schwanthaler

King Ludwig I of Bavaria

King Ludwig I was the father of nine children including the later King Maximilian II (who was the father of King "Kini" Ludwig II) and Otto Friedrich von Wittelsbach, who later became king of Greece. Otto's reign in Greece meant that for a while, the Bavarian Beer Purity Law was in effect there. The Greek flag, which was introduced by Otto, has the Bavarian colors of white and blue to this day, and there is an indisputable spiritual kinship

between Bavaria and Greece—both being said to have qualities like stubbornness, geniality, common sense, and wariness. In Greece, there is an important saying, the message of which is well-known to every Bavarian: "Fassuli, Fassuli, je missito Sakkuli"—"The sack is filled one bean at a time." In Bavarian they say "A bisserl was geht oiwei"—"A little bit goes far."

drafted the first sketches of the statue of Bavaria, the patron of Bavaria, who holds a wreath of oak leaves in her left hand and a sword in her right. A bear pelt is sewn into her robe and she is accompanied by a lion. Historians still debate what these attributes are supposed to mean.

The lion in particular causes many scholarly headaches. Does it stand for the military power of Bavaria, or is it simply a heraldic symbol? The 1860 Munich gymnastics club had nothing to do with it, since it was created ten years after the statue was dedicated. (For your information: Munich's famous soccer team, FC Bayern, was founded in 1900.) At any rate, the Bavaria statue was poured on Erzgießereistraße under the supervision of the bronze caster Johann Baptist Stiglmaier. Although the Ruhmeshalle was not yet finished (it was dedicated three years later), the statue was dedicated with much celebration on October 9, 1850.

Stupidly, by that time King Ludwig I of Bavaria was no longer king. He had gone too far. In 1844 (34 years after the first Oktoberfest) he planned to raise beer prices by a penny. The people had put up with a rise in bread prices, but the news of a possible rise in beer prices was too much. On the very same evening, over two thousand people stormed the breweries, inns, and beer cellars;

helped themselves to the good beer; and smashed everything to bits. The beer revolution had begun. The military was notified immediately but showed solidarity with the uprising and declined to intervene. A few days later the king reversed the increase and actually planned to cut beer prices in the future to "provide the military and the working class with a cheap and healthy drink." (In 1995 history repeated itself when 25,000 citizens of Munich took to the streets and successfully protested an earlier last call in beer gardens.) Munich residents can put up with a lot, but not when it comes to beer.

After this beer rebellion, the king again earned the ire of the people through his scandalous affair with the Irish dancer Lola Montez, eventually leading to

Ludwig's abdication. He left the throne and the dedication of the Bavaria statue to his firstborn son, Maximilian II of Bavaria. If the people of Munich had known how important Oktoberfest would become for their city, they may have been a bit friendlier to poor Ludwig I.

Over the years, new attractions came to Oktoberfest and it became larger and larger. More and more carnival owners came and within a short time there were countless swings, carousels, jungle gyms, lotteries, and

Copycats

Due to the growing popularity of the Munich Oktoberfest, there are countless copycats. Asia, Canada, the USA, Australia, Brazil, Austria, and many other countries have their own Oktoberfests, some half authentic, some completely off the mark. Even in Germany there are imitations such as the Cannstatter Volksfest (colloquially called the "Wasen"), which appeared for the first time eight years after Oktoberfest, in 1818. There is no point in comparing it to Oktoberfest,

but I've been there and I can absolutely recommend it as a lovely, decent folk festival. Among others, there is also a well-attended Oktoberfest in Hannover, a Theresienfest in Hildburgausen, Thuringia, and a Wandsbeker Wies'n in Hamburg. Not Wiesn—the apostrophe matters!

puppet shows starring the traditional character Kasper. Not quite "Olympic," but lovely. The people loved it, at any rate. It was soon clear what people in Munich meant when they said "I'm going to the Wiesn" in October. They were going to enjoy the delights of Oktoberfest on the Theresienwiese.

In 1881 the first Oktoberfest chicken appeared, and the simple beer booths grew into beer halls. Over time everything was improved and renewed. At some point electricity was installed. These days there is also heat. But no technological advances can dampen the essential core of Oktoberfest. Oktoberfest has always preserved its originality.

Why Is It in September?

Oktoberfest was actually originally in October. Because the weather is often really very unpleasant in that month, finding a better solution was debated at length. By 1828 they had already proposed moving the start date one week earlier. The city council, then as now a tough audience, denied the proposal, since the fields around the Theresienwiese would still be in use for farming, and they didn't want to affect the farmers' harvest. At the time, the festival was already beloved and shoes were sturdy, so the fear that the crops could be trampled was valid. St. Petrus apparently disapproved of this unfortunate decision by the city council, since it poured rain every year during Oktoberfest. One year a snowstorm even raged over the Theresienwiese, and a sensible solution was needed. The mills in Bavaria grind more slowly than in other places, so nearly 50 years and many all-night winter debates in well-heated back rooms of Munich inns passed before they brought themselves to turn the Theresienwiese and the surrounding fields into building sites and immediately move Oktoberfest to end on the first Sunday in October.

Now everything was much better and the kegs could be tapped in the middle of September. Traditionally, the kegs are tapped on a Saturday and closed on a Sunday. However, in 1989, the Chancellor happened to set the Day of German Unity on October 3, the anniversary of the death of his mentor, Franz Joseph Strauß—one year after his passing—the Oktoberfest committee decide to make those two extra days into a great Oktoberfest finale. Since then, this is the rule: when the third of October is on a Monday or Tuesday, Oktoberfest will be extended by one or two days. So Oktoberfest lasts at least sixteen days and ideally eighteen days.

"There are many rumors about the climate of Munich, some quite fatal."
Munich Tourist, 1863

One could believe that God loves Oktoberfest. That's why St. Petrus usually makes the sun shine and the beer garden workers rejoice along with the customers who find the mood in the tent a bit too intense. Things are a little more civilized in the beer garden. You have to go without the background music, but in exchange there is fresh air,

Smoking under the Blue and White Sky

As of 2010, you are officially no longer allowed to smoke inside the beer tents. For many, this was unimaginable, but then the self-promoting leader of a minor, irrelevant political party got the idea to lead a reform. Hardly anyone took it seriously, so the voter turnout was very low. The result: a smoking ban in all of Bavaria. Even at Oktoberfest. The problem is that, first of all, it affects the good mood when people have to get up over and over to smoke, and second of all, many have the bad luck of being shut out of the tent because it reached capacity while they were smoking. The tent owners didn't just stand around, they created  good alternatives. For example, in the Winzerer Fähndl you can relax with a cigarette on a lovely balcony with a view of the beautiful fairgrounds and the Bavaria statue—as long as you've made your reservation for the front gallery. Nonsmokers are also welcome on this balcony. Aside from that, there are usually small, blocked-off smoking areas behind or next to the tents.

just as long as you don't sit at a table with long-established cigar smokers. Those smart-aleck health advocates have not yet been able to ban smoking outside, and we wish for the smokers that they never do. Smoking at Oktoberfest has become difficult for those sitting inside the tents. If you want to enjoy tobacco, you must do it in front of the tent. There are also other alternatives such as smoking balconies, since as we remember: a little bit goes far.

Arrival and Orientation

Getting There

It is best to use public transportation or to walk. In general, cars are great, but you can never find parking near Oktoberfest, and anyway, if you drive, you can't drink. Not drinking is often a good idea, but at Oktoberfest it's out-and-out nonsense.

The U-Bahn

If you don't know your way around Munich, your best bet is to take U-Bahn line U4 or U5 to the "Theresienwiese" stop. Coming south from the center of the city, you arrive directly in the heart of Oktoberfest. Because many people know this, this exit is often overcrowded, so you can use the north exit instead. According to my exhaustive research, no one has missed Oktoberfest that way yet.

Those who know the city a little bit can take the U3 or U6 to "Goetheplatz" or "Poccistraße" instead. It's just a short hike from there. Coming from the west, the U-Bahn stop "Schwanthalerhöhe" on the U4 or U5 line is a good choice. From here, just follow the crowd. Don't worry: they're all going to Oktoberfest.

The S-Bahn

The S-Bahn also stops near Oktoberfest, specifically at "Hackerbrücke." This station is between the main station (Hauptbahnhof) and the "Donnersbergerbrücke" stop and is serviced by all S-Bahn lines. From Hackerbrücke you only have to walk a few minutes to Oktoberfest. Here, too: simply follow the current of people. If there is no crowd to follow, then you have made a mistake with your compass, your watch, or your calendar.

The Tram

You can also get to Oktoberfest on tram lines 18 and 19. It's best to get off at the "Hermann-Lingg-Straße" stop. As always: just follow the crowd.

There's space everywhere for cozy togetherness.

All roads lead to the beer tent.

RVs

During Oktoberfest, the streets around the Wiesn are not open to RVs, and camping out on the street, though it sounds enticing, is not allowed in the entire city. The police patrol constantly—really! Parking spaces with sanitary facilities for about a thousand RVs are available in eastern Munich on the De-Gasperi-Bogen on the Riem fairground. From there you can travel to Oktoberfest easily on public transportation.

Cars

One more time to be sure: leave your car parked at home. Firstly, because you don't want to drink and drive, and secondly, because you'll never find a parking spot.

Taxis

Taxi drivers around Oktoberfest don't often put their lights on so that they can check how intoxicated their potential customers are and whether to expect unfortunate surprises. This behavior seems outrageous, but after many years witnessing drunken riders, the author finds it completely understandable. What is really reprehensible is those taxi drivers who decide that someone's trip is not profitable enough, and refuse them a ride. These taxi drivers should be reported to the dispatcher if you can still articulate clearly. Well-dressed couples are usually picked up; they have a reputation of rarely causing problems.

Rickshaws

Bicycle rickshaws are fun and you get to stay out in the fresh air. But be careful! Many rickshaw drivers shamelessly charge exorbitant fares. Not all, but many. You should know how far your destination is and discuss a fair price in advance which you are prepared to pay. Better to walk than pay 50 euros for half a mile of travel.

Handicapped Parking

There are about a hundred handicapped parking spots in the southern part of the Theresienwiese, with an entrance on Stielerstraße. The vehicles of aid organizations should drive over the Anlieferstraße WEST behind the Hippodrom tent.

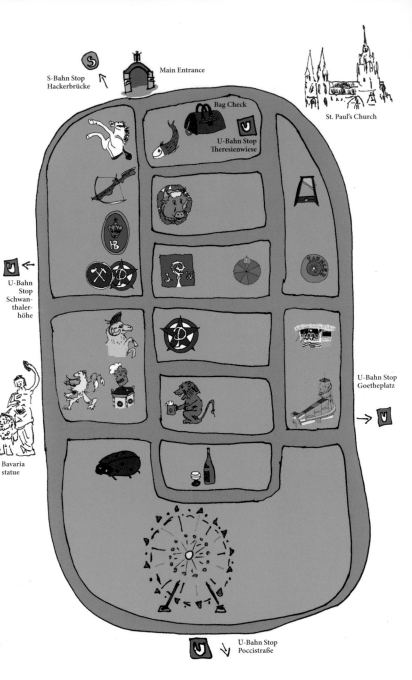

S-Bahn Stop
Hackerbrücke

Main Entrance

Bag Check

U-Bahn Stop
Theresienwiese

St. Paul's Church

U-Bahn
Stop
Schwan-
thaler-
höhe

U-Bahn Stop
Goetheplatz

Bavaria
statue

U-Bahn Stop
Poccistraße

Beer Tents

 Hippodrom

 Käfer's Wies'n-Schänke

 Armbrust-schützenzelt

 Fischer-Vroni

 Hofbrau-Festzelt

 Ochsenbraterei

 Hacker-Festzelt

 Augustiner-Festhalle

 Festhalle Schottenhamel

 Festhalle Pschorr-Bräurosl

 Schützen-Festzelt

 Löwenbräu-Festzelt

 Winzerer Fähndl

 Kuffler's Weinzelt

Attractions

 Schichtl's Variety Show

 Krinoline (Carousel)

 Teufelsrad (Devil's Wheel)

 Toboggan (Slide)

 Taumler (Tilt-a-Whirl)

 Riesenrad (Ferris Wheel)

What Is Where and Where Am I?

The structure of Oktoberfest is generally very clear and well laid-out. There are two large entrances to be found on the northern ends of the two large lanes of Oktoberfest:

The main entrance with the "Willkommen zum Oktoberfest" gate is at the beginning of Wirtsbudenstraße —colloquially known as "Zeltstraße" ("Tent Street"), "Bierstraße" ("Beer Street") or "Biergasse" ("Beer Lane"), because that's where the beer is—which is lined on either side with just about every important festival tent.

The southern exit of the Theresienwiese U-Bahn stop is at the beginning of Schaustellerstraße—colloquially known as "Schaubudengasse" ("Booth Lane"), "Fahrgeschäftestraße" ("Ride Street"), or "Sensations-gasse" ("Sensation Lane") to the locals—which runs about 500 feet parallel to Wirtsbudenstraße. Here you can find

Nothing would work without me.

carousels, bumper cars, haunted houses, and roller coasters. On Schaustellerstraße there are also schnapps stands, which can't be found on Wirtsbudenstraße.

To sum up: after the main entrance there is food and beer, and parallel to that, attractions and schnapps.

Lost and Found

So that you don't lose anything important on the Wiesn (and that happens very quickly), it makes sense to either leave all your valuables at home or to check them at the bag check at the beginning of your Oktoberfest visit. There is a bag check directly to the right of the southern

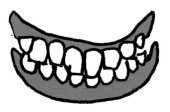

exit of the Theresienwiese U-Bahn stop; that is the front of the train if you are coming from the center of the city. You can also check strollers here.

And if something goes missing anyway, it might be turned into the Wiesnfundamt (Oktoberfest Lost and Found). That's where you bring found items. Every year, thousands of items are turned in and often picked up: dentures, cell phones, wallets, keys, bras, card games, flashlights, backpacks, musical instruments, and countless other items that can be easily forgotten in the beer tent, next to the bumper cars, or on the Ferris wheel.

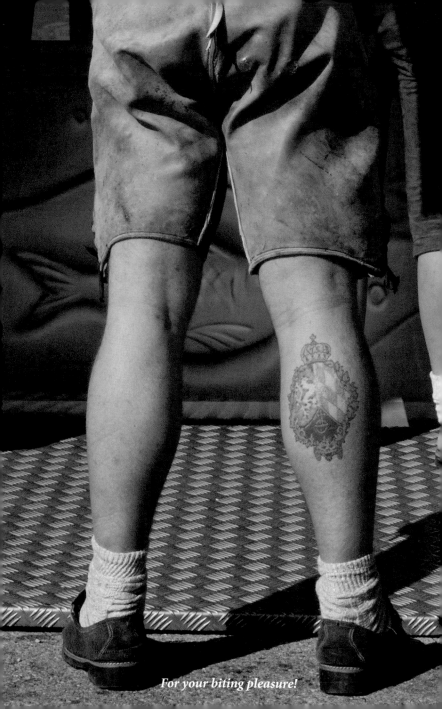

For your biting pleasure!

Unless you suffer from chronic listlessness or claustrophobia, there is a guaranteed thrill to be found here for every woman, man, grandma, grandpa, girl, and boy. Wirtsbudenstraße and Schaustellerstraße are connected via five clearly laid-out lanes. And so, in a sense, the Wiesn is a portable chess board of happiness.

Who Else Is There?

Visitors from every country on earth stream into Oktoberfest, which we like because for one, we are a very hospitable people, and for another, we enjoy when others are interested in our customs. So don't be shy; we don't bite. Quite the opposite. In Bavaria everyone addresses each other informally, except for authority figures. I call everyone

"Sie" versus "Du"

Throughout the world, people typically use given names or nicknames when speaking to close friends, family members, and even friendly business associates. The last name is generally used only in formal relationships. In the German-speaking parts of the world, there are two different words equivalent to the English word "you"—"*du*" is used in personal address and "*sie*" in formal speech. "Du" signals social proximity, empathy, intimacy. "Sie" shows social distance, neutrality, and respect.

The only way to get rid of a temptation is to yield to it.
Oscar Wilde (1854–1900)

"du" and have rarely gone to court over it. It simplifies everything and gives a familiar tone to conversations.

Where people are drinking good beer, the atmosphere is welcoming. People joke, laugh, and chat. Interpersonal relations are finally relaxed. People are always flirting, and especially at Oktoberfest. If you're not trying, something will happen anyway. And if you're trying, it will, too.

Now there are many different kinds of people at Oktoberfest to chat and flirt with. So that you can get along a little better, I've summed up the most important groups:

The Natives

Many Munich natives go to the Löwenbräu or Hacker tents. It's best to meet people outside the tent in the beer garden, where it's more peaceful and where you can have a better conversation over the quieter music. You can tell the locals by their contented expressions, slightly plump figures, and their healthy, sometimes quite pink faces, as well as their friendly but difficult to understand, sometimes crotchety-seeming jabber. Some have a beard, sometimes styled, and some smoke cigars. They often wear Tracht, but so do very many people at Oktoberfest, so that doesn't tell you if someone's a native. Female locals are mostly very attractive, laugh a lot, and are captivating with a stunning, natural charm.

How to flirt: just approach them boldly, and either it works or it doesn't. You'll lose out if you hesitate too long or beat around the bush.

Other German-Speaking Visitors

Oktoberfest attracts drinkers from all corners of Germany. They often wear Tracht—which is good—but they usually speak differently than Bavarians. It's usually very amusing since a Saxon in lederhosen certainly has his own charm. Since we in Bavaria have aligned all our thoughts and deeds with "live and let live," everyone is accepted. We're all equal

41

Dolce far niente . . .

in the beer tent.

How to flirt: if someone speaks a strange dialect, they don't at all like to talk about it. To keep it in the realm of flirting and not debate, it is a good idea to avoid political themes of all types.

Italians

Particularly during the second weekend, about a quarter million Italians travel to Oktoberfest. It seems that they like to travel all together. On Thursday it begins, and on Sunday it ends. Italian after Italian. Travel agencies on the other side of the Alps begin offering custom all-inclusive tours months in advance. Italians often travel in large, closed groups, but like everyone else at Oktoberfest can be easily befriended.

How to flirt: knowing a few Italian phrases can't go amiss. A good sentence, for example, is "Vorrei un po di piu schiuma sulla mia birra," which means "I would like a little more foam on my beer." It will make most Italians laugh. And laughter opens the portal to the heart.

Asians

In the author's experience, many Asians also enjoy Oktoberfest tradition, Tracht, and music, as well as the old-fashioned Bavarian traditions. Like with most people at the festival, you can have fun Oktoberfest afternoons and evenings together.

How to flirt: Asians at Oktoberfest tend to be shy in the author's experience. It's easy to start a conversation, but hard to flirt. It never hurts to try a few fast-paced drinking games that you remember from your school days.

Other English-Speaking Visitors

People from Australia, Canada, America, New Zealand, England, Ireland, and Scotland all love Oktoberfest. For some unknown reason, some guests from the English-speaking world think that Oktoberfest is like Karnival

and dress up in full-body animal costumes or wigs. At any rate, English-speakers love to celebrate, so they fit right in at Oktoberfest.

How to flirt: Since the English-speaking guests are rather jolly and euphoric, it is very easy to start a conversation with them. They come to Oktoberfest to have fun, so flirting is uncomplicated.

VIPs

You mostly meet stars in the Käfer Wies'n-Schänke and the Hippodrom, but sporadically also in the wine tent and in the Winzerer Fähndl. As far as possible, don't just strike up conversation with celebs, since VIPs would also like to enjoy Oktoberfest in peace and don't love being bothered by strangers during their private visit. But you are allowed to look.

How to flirt: if you find yourself at a table with a celebrity, you've been dealt a good hand. If you're sitting at a different table, not so much. You have to be a little careful with flirting here, since lots of people want to flirt with a star, even at Oktoberfest. Oktoberfest beer is not only delicious, but also very euphoric. It's better to practice restraint. If the VIP wants to flirt of their own accord, you'll know.

Scalpers, Scammers, and Con Artists

It's not only nice people that come to Oktoberfest. That must be said clearly. Everyone has to be careful in life, and particularly when intoxicated. But many crooks have discovered that Oktoberfest is a playground with easy prey for them. It is particularly important to always keep an eye on your valuables since they're easy game for pickpockets in the crowded turmoil. Furthermore, there are other stories, such as when a shady figure approaches you in front of a full tent with the words, "I'll get you in for 20 euros." Don't fall for their lines!

How to flirt: scalpers, scammers, and con artists don't want to flirt; they want to rip you off. Friends of mine from Schleswig-Holstein were once brought to a tent entrance that was open anyway by one of these scammers. And of course he kept the money for his service. A tourist from Norway once told me how he and a friend had paid one of these "service providers" 100 euros, who told them to wait by the entrance for him to get them. He was let in because of his reservation bracelet and was never seen again. A lovely and very attractive friend of mine told me how she was standing broken-hearted at a barrier, having missed a cutoff. She had decided to return home with a heavy heart when a security guard spoke to her. "Would you like to get into the tent?" She was happily surprised, and said yes. The man brought her to the back of the tent into an employees-only side entrance. When they got inside, he said to my friend: "You can come in, but only if you take off your panties in front of me and give them to me." That wasn't flirting, but sexual assault. She walked out indignantly and with good luck, was able to get into the tent later. Along with her underwear.

The Police
The police at Oktoberfest have a hard job, and their orders are to be followed without complaint. They keep a cool head even in extreme situations and give friendly advice to visitors' questions. This deserves a certain respect, since it is surely not always easy to deal with unreasonable drunks. However, the Munich Police have a good grip on things. Sometimes they have things in an armlock, but then it's quickly peaceful again.

Very important: you should avoid fighting at Oktoberfest, since it does no good and no one needs it. Oktoberfest is a friendly place, the beer lifts your mood and calms your mind, and you should only conduct a healthy self-assessment as needed to know how much you can tolerate. Of course there are occasional disputes here and there, in which you shouldn't get involved if you don't have to. Better to leave that to the

Say it with flowers.

police and security guards, who can arbitrate or, when in doubt, send people away.

How to flirt: since the keepers of the peace are there professionally and not privately, you should just let them do their work and not flirt with them. That goes for everyone who is at Oktoberfest on business.

Emergency Personnel

Paramedics, doctors, and EMS are available everywhere at Oktoberfest and are ready to help in an instant if someone gets hurt. If there's a rescue team called to action, it is best to make room for them to get by and let them get to work. There's enough to see at Oktoberfest that there's no need to get in the way of rescue workers giving first aid. You can help by just stepping to the side.

"Just take these antacids, and then you'll be ready for the beer tent again."

How to flirt: Intentionally passing out so that you can get mouth-to-mouth from a paramedic has been done. Calling out "Do you come here often?" to emergency medical personnel won't have a very positive result, either. In this case let people do their work and look for someone who is there in a private capacity, instead.

Clothing

Traditional Garb (*Tracht*), Jeans, or a Bunny Costume?

In general, there is no dress code at Oktoberfest. One hundred years ago, people wore simple and sturdy clothing that was OK to get dirty. Back then, clothing at Oktoberfest was traditional, but not stylish. Today it's different. About 70 percent of visitors show up in *Tracht* (or at least outfits reminiscent of Tracht). Unfortunately, many visitors believe that Oktoberfest is similar to Fasching or Karnival, and show up in bunny costumes, togas, or as Spiderman. You should avoid this if at all possible, because it simply doesn't belong in a beer tent. Once I saw a lost member of a stag party wearing an exceptionally outlandish costume consisting of a gold princess tiara, a silver cloak, and a frilly shirt that was already quite dirty. He

Looks good from behind, too.

Clothes off the rack.

was sitting, alone and forgotten, next to a merry crowd. If the server hadn't taken pity on him and sold him a glass so that he could join in the toasting, he would probably have perished from loneliness.

To the point: either you go in Tracht, or in plainclothes—jeans or, if you want, in a jacket. But since Bavaria has such lovely traditions—and such lovely clothing to go along with them—everyone should give it a try and not pass up an opportunity to wear Tracht. And where is it more appropriate than Oktoberfest?

The word "Tracht" comes from the word "Tragen," "to wear," and referred to the clothing worn in the country and cities. Over the centuries, unique kinds of Trachten developed in the Alps. According to social standing and ancestry, everyone wore quite different pants, jackets, skirts, vests, shoes, and hats. They were also differentiated by duchy, kingdom, or other sovereign territory. Some rulers released clothing decrees dictating which items of clothing farmers, farmhands, merchants, and even children had to wear and, even more drastically, were not allowed to wear due to their low status. After the French Revolution in 1789, this practice fell into decline. Just a few years later, Trachten came into fashion in Bavaria in a big way. The Bavarian historian Felix Joseph Freiherr von Lipowsky is known today as one of the biggest trendsetters of the Trachten movement. In 1830 he published the book *Sammlung Bayerischer National-Costume* ("A Compilation of Bavarian National Costume") and with that, he started a downright euphoric wave of Trachten popularity.

In essence, it was the same back then as it is now: women wear dirndls and men wear lederhosen. (True, since Tracht enthusiasts like to be cheeky and a bit provocative, the recent trend of women wearing lederhosen is logical and completely in line. However, I do hope that it never comes into fashion for men to go around in dirndls.) Classic Bavarian Tracht appears in six different forms: Berchtesgadener, Chiemgadener, Inntaler, Isarwinkler, Miesbacher,

Show us your calves!

and Werdenfelser. In addition, there are countless regional styles from all possible and impossible corners of Austria and Bavaria. Wearing Tracht always goes along with a strong connection to one's homeland and with the Bavarian way of life. People often used to wear Tracht in their everyday lives, but today they wear it predominantly for festive occasions. It's nice when people from outside the Alps wear our traditional clothing, but you absolutely must be aware that wearing Tracht is not a costume—your heart must be in it.

Men's Clothing

Lederhosen

There are "Bundlederne" (lederhosen that gather below the knee) and "Kurze" (short lederhosen that expose the knees). The simplest are made from pig leather, which hardens quickly and is difficult to care for and therefore not recommended. Better lederhosen are made from cow leather, even better from deer leather, and the best from chamois leather, although you have to be careful since it is not very sturdy and tears easily.

Lederhosen have a flap in the front which can be opened quickly by a man to answer the call of nature (or for totally different reasons). When the need arises, women can open the flap on a man's pants just as quickly. The buttons are designed for quick access from above or in front. On the right side (as seen from above) of

Beer is proof that God loves us and wants us to be happy.
Benjamin Franklin (1706–1790)

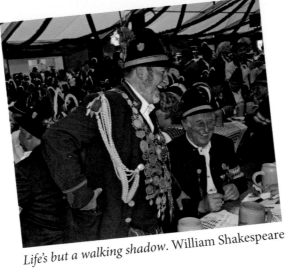

Life's but a walking shadow. William Shakespeare

each pair of lederhosen there is a knife pouch, where you would traditionally keep your hunting knife. Since knives aren't allowed at Oktoberfest for safety reasons, you should find something else to put in there in this case. When the police come by on their patrol, they will take your knife away, and it will be very difficult to get it back. That's why when I'm at Oktoberfest I keep useful things in my knife pouch such as a flashlight, a fountain pen, or a thermometer to measure the temperature.

Many lederhosen have suspenders that are kept stable by a strap across the chest. Embellishments and embroidery depend on the origin of the lederhosen. You can wear lederhosen without suspenders as long as you are built so that they won't slip. That really looks stupid and it significantly hinders walking. Some modern lederhosen have belt loops. I strongly recommend that when you are choosing your belt, you go with a belt buckle appropriate to the occasion, for example the face of King Ludwig II, or a simple Tracht belt.

If you've done it right you should look wild, rustic, and bold in your lederhosen. Don't part your hair, let it be a bit messy, and open the top button of your shirt.

Tracht Belts

As a rule, a Tracht belt is a rustic leather belt with embellishments and embroidery. It is worn over the Tracht, be it lederhosen, a bodice, a skirt, or a blouse. It will usually have an artfully deco-  rated buckle with shields, deer, edelweiss, or other Alpine themes. There are also Tracht belts with Charivari, or silver decorations, worked in.

Old lederhosen are better than new, since they have to be broken in to have the right fit. A solid color or checked shirt with deer antler buttons works best with lederhosen. I personally prefer white or beige socks, not pulled up tightly but rather casually pushed down a little. You

Calves

One aspect of Bavarian dress is calves. You acquire them by hiking in the mountains, riding bikes, lifting weights, and working the land. Both ladies and gentlemen should have respectable calves. If you don't have any, there's a solution for you: The Munich lederhosen king, Herbert Lipah, has invented the "Wadl-Wadl" or "Calf-calf." It's a shapely calf made of foam rubber that comes in two different models: the King's calf and the sweet calf. More information is at www.wadlwadl.de.

are free to wear socks in other colors, of course, but please no pink or neon green ones. Like I said, this is Oktoberfest and not Karnival.

The Care of Lederhosen

You must care for your lederhosen by hanging them up so they can breathe. You can also carefully stick a broad, good quality piece of tape to them and then quickly pull it off. This is very good for getting rid of fuzz and grease spots.

You can also wash your lederhosen, but it is a very laborious process. They should be hand washed in a good amount of lukewarm suds with a lot of soft soap leather cleaner added. Repeat several times, and then rinse with fresh water mixed with fresh soft soap. As long as you use enough of the leather soft soap, the lederhosen won't lose any of their necessary oils. Finally, squeeze out the excess water without scrunching up the leather, and lay the lederhosen out on a towel. Under no circumstances should you lay them out in the sun or in a heated room, or else they will dry out. With each washing, the lederhosen will inevitably lose some of their natural coloring, so consider that before you wash them. Drying the lederhosen requires just one short week, during which you should turn and bend them into all different positions as well as pull the pockets inside out once a day. If the lederhosen are too stiff after drying, they can be very carefully kneaded until they are soft again. Afterwards, oil them with leather oil, preferably brushed on thinly with a paintbrush. Then hang them up. They must hang for another week, but then they will bring you lots of joy once again. If you don't have time or are not very good at laundry, you can also get yourself a goat. Or so I've heard. It will lick the lederhosen clean because it thinks there is high-quality, mineral-rich salt in them. Sometimes the animal is right, but sometimes not. In any case, the lederhosen will be thoroughly clean. But now I'll knock it off with the goat, so that we don't descend into nonsense.

Charivari

A Charivari is a large, silver chain attached to lederhosen or a Tracht vest. It is hung with animal teeth, paws, coins, metal decorations, badger fur, and precious stones. Charivari means something like "jumble."

The Costume and Riflemen's Procession

To honor the silver wedding anniversary of King Ludwig I and his Therese, there is a big parade every first Sunday of Oktoberfest at 9:30 a.m. It is made up of over 150 traditionally dressed groups with over 9,000 participants from all over Europe. They present folk dances, Tracht fashions, and shooting clubs. At the front of the procession the Münchner Kindl, the Oktoberfest mascot from the Munich  coat of arms, waves to the excited viewers lining the path to the Theresienwiese. It starts at the Maximilianeum, goes down Maximilianstraße and Residenzstraße, past the Bavarian State Opera built by Ludwig II for Richard Wagner, over to Odeonsplatz, through Karlsplatz straight to Schwanthalerstraße, left around the corner into Paul-Heyse-Straße, which leads more or less straight to Oktoberfest. More information is at www.festring-muenchen.de.

Haferl Shoes

The best shoes to go with Bavarian lederhosen are Haferl shoes. They are traditionally made from black nappa leather. Variations made of suede or other good leather are completely acceptable. You should made sure that the inside leather is soft so that the shoe is comfortable and doesn't get uncomfortable with hard wearing. Guys should wear sturdy shoes with a wide sole and a strong  profile. For the youngsters in the past, the path to the dance floor often went through puddles and rocks, so the shoes should be able to withstand the today's stresses. Because you just never know.

Women's Clothing

Dirndls

The traditional Alpine dress for women is called the "dirndl." Originally, the dirndl was a costume for servants in lordly households, but over time it was worn more and more by women in the Alpine regions and summer visitors for private and festive occasions. If we are being particular, I must explain that we cannot exactly equate dirndls with highly complex Alpine folk costume. Here I am concerned with pretty dirndls that you can see at Oktoberfest.

A rose is a rose is a rose . . .

Ideally, a dirndl should be very comfortable, without much fuss and neatly laced up. Whether short or long, historic or modern, everything pretty and not vulgar is allowed. But please, no dirndls in leopard print or from the newest Barbie collection. Preferably they should be one or two colors. Simple, flat shoes and crocheted stockings are worn with a dirndl. Haferl shoes, simple pumps, or ballet flats will work in a pinch—under no circumstances should you wear flip flops or black pleather boots laced up to your chin.

A dirndl consists of a linen or fine cotton "Schmisl" (blouse) in a subtle color with gathered or puffed sleeves and a round or square neckline that can be chaste or allow for a "better look," as you prefer. Over the blouse is the "Mieder" or "Leibl" (the actual dirndl dress) made from linen, silk, or cotton. Usually there is a pocket on the side or front of the skirt which is hidden under the obligatory apron. There are also two-piece dirndls which allow for countless combinations, since the skirt and bodice are separate. You should wear the bodice tight enough that there are no wrinkles, but not too tight—it should look pretty, not keep you from breathing. (You can experiment with tight bodices in one of those clubs where people whip each other, but not at Oktoberfest or other festive events.) The simpler it is, the more lovely and attractive. Many dirndls have nice lacing. The Mieder used to be laced up from bottom to top with a silver chain. Today it is usually closed

Wear your dirndl for yodeling.

with a small chain or simply a zipper hidden by the lacing. The silver chain is decorated with coins and amulets. Women also like to wear a matching shawl over their shoulders—preferably artfully embroidered with a small pattern. A choker with a nice pendant is a better accessory than a bunch of necklaces which will fly up around your ears on the roller coaster. The high-waisted, pleated dirndl skirt is usually ankle length. A petticoat gives it the right volume, keeps it from gathering between your legs, and looks nice when it peeks out from underneath. If your skirt must be short, it should at least cover your knees. Only shepherdesses who don't want to trip while climbing mountains have a good excuse to wear their skirts any shorter. The strength of the dirndl doesn't lie in bare legs, but rather in the lovely décolletage. Nothing should distract from that. There are generally very few real color rules when it comes to a dirndl. It shouldn't be too gaudy, but rather a subtle color such as light blue or pink. Black with a white blouse is uncommon, since it used to be the color worn by servants. A tasteful dirndl, with fine embroidery, well-tailored darts, and pretty buttons, enhances a woman's natural beauty; a baggy, beige farmhouse dirndl that fits like a sack or a garish Christmas candy-colored dirndl, on the other hand, do not.

The Care of Dirndls

It is best to have your dirndl washed for you since it saves you work and gets a better result. If you don't have a cleaner near you, you can improve the smell with a bunch of lavender, though that won't make it clean. If you would like to wash your dirndl yourself, it is best to wash the dress (or bodice and skirt) separately, inside out in a lingerie bag, on a cold gentle cycle. This will keep the color from fading. The blouse and apron should also be washed separately in lingerie bags. Do not put them in the dryer, but rather dry them in the shower or outside on a wooden drying rack, still inside out. Finally, iron while making sure that the pleats are lying correctly. It is also a good idea to store your dirndl in a clothing bag made of breathable fabric in the off-season.

When There's a Spot on Your Dirndl

Of course, it all depends on the origin of the spot. Many spots can be removed with cold water and gall soap. Only use hot water in special cases, since it will cause many stains to solidify and just get more entrenched in the fabric. Burn marks should be moistened and then sprinkled with salt. Red wine spots can be dealt with the same way. The salt pulls the spot out of the fabric. If you  are using gall soap, please remember: good dirndls are made of good materials, so it is a good idea to test the colorfastness in a hidden spot before you wash with the soap. Wax spots can be removed with blotting paper and an iron. If gum has been caught in your dirndl, it should be frozen. The frozen gum can easily be scratched off.

Aprons and Bows

The "Bow Code" has been around for a few years. It may come from the American tradition of the "Hanky Code," where gay men advertise their sexual interests by wearing different colored hankies on different places on their bodies.

Dirndl bows are used in a similar way. You can read the marital status of a lady in the bow of her dirndl apron. If the bow is tied in the back, she is a widow. Otherwise it should be tied in the front. If the bow is on the right, the girl is engaged, married, or otherwise spoken for—that means hands off! If the bow is on the left, the lady's heart is yet to be won, and she is free to be approached. If the bow is tied in front center, either she is still a virgin or she hasn't heard of the secret language of apron bows.

Headwear and the Wildbart

If you arrive at Oktoberfest feeling euphoric, as is to be expected, you can also express your high spirits by choosing cheerful hat. If it doesn't feel too idiotic for you to run around with a plush beer stein or some shapeless felt mat on your head, then feel free. It's not my thing. A good alternative is a classic Tracht hat, which are available in all price ranges and quality levels, and always look good.

In addition, I am a big fan of the Wildbart. Why not go whole hog? A Wildbart is a traditional hat decoration for men. It is worn in combination with Tracht, on top of the hat. It is made of hair

We make a virtue out of necessity.

from a badger, deer, boar, or chamois, bound together at one end so that the loose hair can puff out in a bushy, round shape. The most famous kind of Wildbart is the Gamsbart, made from hair from the back of a chamois. The tips of the hair must be light so that there is a "frost" that makes the Gamsbart shimmer at the end.

But be careful: a Wildbart is a high-quality and very expensive accessory, and you should take enough time (and money) when choosing one. A scruffy shaving brush on your Tracht hat is not Gamsbart, no matter which way you turn it.

For women, appropriate headwear is fancy braids, headbands, stylish hats with or without feathers, or other options. Historical Trachten are often combined with a

The braid show.

hat, even for women. Don't be shy; getting all done up isn't against the rules!

Where Do I Buy Trachten?

Around Oktoberfest time, many Munich clothing stores begin selling lederhosen, Trachten, dirndls, Haferl shoes, mountain boots, socks, and Trachten accessories. If you don't know your stuff, it's a good idea to bring along an "expert" so that you don't get taken in or end up going home with a T-shirt printed with lederhosen suspenders. Prices vary as with all textiles, and are dependent on brand, material, and decoration. It's better to spend a bit more and buy something sensible that can be enjoyed for a long time, than to try to get a bargain. The basic uniform for a woman is blouse, dress, bodice, petticoat, and apron; the basic uniform for a man is Tracht shirt, Tracht socks, Haferl shoes, and lederhosen. "Underneath" you should wear nice clean underwear, but please, dear gentlemen, it cannot be repeated often enough: you do not wear an undershirt or T-shirt under a Tracht shirt. It should be worn against your bare skin.

I will share four businesses with you that, in my opinion, sell lovely Trachten fashion:

Angermaier: A name that everyone knows. At Angermaier you will find high-quality and very modern Trachten, by far the most beautiful vests and finest dirndls, and terrific advice. There are two locations in Munich: Rosental 10 and Landsberger Straße 101-103.

www.trachten-angermaier.de

Steindl: Trachten Outlet. Steindl offers simple, predominantly Austrian Trachten fashion for the smaller wallet. It can be found, among other locations, right in the Viktualienmarkt at Rosental 5. If you're lucky, the very knowledgeable and friendly Ramon will give you some advice.

www.wiesn-tracht-mehr.de

Holareidulijö: Holareidulijö sells new and used lederhosen and Trachten, saucy leather dirndls, regional Bavarian Trachten, good mountain boots, accessories, sweaters, loden coats, and Bavarian curiosities at Schellingstraße 81.

www.holareidulijoe.com

Lederhosenwahnsinn: Lederhosenwahnsinn offers a homey Bavarian mood and the biggest selection of secondhand lederhosen in the world, located in the Borstei (Franz-Marc-Straße 10). They also give excellent advice. And if you're friendly and have a bit of time, you'll almost certainly get a beer while you're trying things on.

www.lederhosenwahnsinn.de

Traditional Cuisine—Beer

Oktoberfest Beer

At Oktoberfest, only Munich beers are served. To be specific: the six Munich breweries that are allowed at Oktoberfest (Augustiner, Hacker-Pschorr, Hofb räu, Löwenbräu, Paulaner and Spaten) each brew a special Oktoberfest beer for the Oktoberfest season. It has a slightly higher original gravity (around 13 percent) and thus is has more alcohol (between 5.7 and 6.3 percent) than the regular light Munich lager. Because of this, it's somewhat sweeter and hoppier—and it goes wonderfully with Oktoberfest chicken, roast pork, pork knuckle, and all the other Oktoberfest delicacies. But you have to drink it quickly since it has slightly lower carbonation that only lasts a short time.

The traditional Oktoberfest beer used to be Märzen beer, a "reserve beer" brewed in the spring before it is too warm for brewing and brewed stronger so it could be stored for longer. If the beer reserves ran low at the end of the year, they could pull out the Märzen. These days, some of the beer on offer at Oktoberfest is still called "Märzen," but it is specially brewed for Oktoberfest and

Radler

Radler is a mixture of lemon soda and beer. It is also known as "Alsterwasser." The mixture ratio is usually 1:1, but sometimes it varies. Some people believe that this drink was invented for cyclists who were terribly thirsty between laps and needed a quick beverage. And since cyclists aren't stupid, they always poured some beer into their lemon soda. But that isn't true. There is an urban legend that the owner of the "Kugler Alm" beer garden in Oberhaching near Munich invented the drink in a desperate moment. According to legend, on a sunny after-

noon in 1922 so many cyclists came in and ordered one beer after another that he mixed the beer with lemon soda so that he wouldn't run out, and called it "Radlermaß," or "cyclist beer." That's a good story, but unfortunately it isn't true. The term Radlermaß actually appeared for the first time in the 1912 memoir by Lena Christ, *Memories of a Redundant Person*.

It all depends on beer.

so it must be called "Oktoberfest beer" if you want to be correct. It is served from steel kegs. The only exception is the Augustiner Oktoberfest beer, which is still served in the traditional manner, from wooden barrels.

Beer prices at Oktoberfest are a delicate subject and cause general resentment every year shortly before the festival. Wrongfully so, in my opinion. Since Oktoberfest is free to get into and the proprietors make sure you won't find such a wonderful mixture of amusement and concentrated euphoria anywhere else in the world, it's best not to make a fuss over the beer prices. Instead, save up for Oktoberfest and then spend your time drinking instead of complaining.

A Tasting: The Beers at Oktoberfest

The six Munich Oktoberfest beers are: Augustiner, Paulaner, Hacker-Pschorr, Löwenbräu, Hofbräu, and Spaten. Other kinds of beer may not be served at Oktoberfest, which is a shame because there are other beloved types of Bavarian beer such as the Tegernseer Helle or the beer from the King Ludwig Castle Brewery in Kaltenberg, which once served the court of Oktoberfest founder Ludwig I.

For this book, I had two independent juries taste the six Oktoberfest beers in fall of 2011. I developed a tasting plan with a lot of worth placed on the criteria that are typical of Oktoberfest beer. Since the beer going flat is tied to how quickly the drinker drinks it, I decided to rate the carbonation only during the first half of the beer.

The first team (Brigade A) was composed of just two people, namely a food and beer special- ist from Munich and myself. We tasted the beers on site, in the big tent for each brewery.

Men's accessories.

The Beer Stein

Beer steins were once made of clay; these days they are made of glass. For one, you can ensure that it's always kept full, which is more difficult with a clay mug. For another, you can see the color of the beer and the foam. And, once and for all: don't steal beer steins. Empty them and leave them with their owner.

The second team (Brigade B) was composed of four people: my dear friend Peter Eichhorn (beer expert and

Pour us another!

author of the excellent German handbook of beer *From Ale to Zwickel—The ABCs of Beer*) along with a brewer, a wine sommelier, and the administrator of an internet beer forum. They tasted and compared the 2011 Oktoberfest beers in bottles outside of Oktoberfest.

Each judge in Brigade A and Brigade B knew which beer he was tasting; it was not a blind taste test.

Brigade A: Tasting in the Beer Tent

We began in the beer garden of the Löwenbräu tent (Löwenbräu), worked our way through the Winzerer Fähndl (Paulaner), the Festhalle Schottenhamel (Spaten), the Augustiner Festhalle (Augustiner), the Hacker tent (Hacker-Pschorr), and the Hofbräu tent (Hofbräu), diligently noting our impressions. Since we were very aware that six steins is a lot, we were concerned with the results, and I wanted to rate the carbonation correctly, we only drank a bit more than half of each. We left the rest to fate. Because of our notepads, our neighbors or servers often spoke to us, and we honestly explained that we were doing a taste test.

The next morning I had an unbelievable hangover. I typed up our results, which was not easy since our scribbled-down ratings were not very readable, particularly toward the end of our tour. I was surprised to find that Augustiner, which is the absolute favorite beer of so many people I know, had come off the worst according to our criteria. But everyone has a bad day now and then, even Augustiner Oktoberfest beer. Here are the results:

Marry in haste, repent in leisure …

1ˢᵗ Place: Hacker-Pschorr: Golden brown, slightly cloudy, the foam is uniform with large bubbles, primary scent fruity, secondary scent spicy, scent when swirled just as spicy, round and smooth initial taste, sparkling and balanced carbonation, sour and pleasantly sweet aftertaste.

2ⁿᵈ Place: Hofbräu: Light yellow color, bubbly foam that disappears quickly, primary scent too hoppy, secondary scent balanced fruitiness, scent when swirled just as fruity, round and pleasantly tart initial taste, short-lived carbonation, pleasantly bitter and light aftertaste.

3ʳᵈ Place: Paulaner: Light yellow, clear, fine foam, primary scent spicy, secondary scent drops off somewhat, fermented smell when swirled, pleasantly bitter initial taste, relatively fresh, relatively long-lived carbonation, hoppy aftertaste.

4ᵗʰ Place: Spaten: Amber colored, clear, the foam disappears quickly, hoppy primary scent, fruity secondary scent, scent when swirled is sweetish, bittersweet initial taste, short-lived carbonation, aftertaste is too light, but pleasantly bitter.

> **5th Place: Löwenbräu:** Light brown, clear, fine foam that disappears quickly, primary scent malty, secondary scent of fermentation, spicy scent when swirled, pleasantly bitter initial taste, initially balanced carbonation which disappears quickly, bittersweet aftertaste.
>
> **6th Place: Augustiner:** Yellow-gold, clear, creamy foam, primary and secondary scents of fermentation and a bit of wooden barrel, scent when swirled is spicy, initial taste is too alcoholic, goes flat quickly, aftertaste is too sweet and, just as in the beginning, too strong.

I then waited excitedly for the results from my beer pros in Brigade B, who tasted the beers out of bottles.

Delicious!

Brigade B: Tasting out of Bottles

The four testers of Brigade B met in a peaceful, private place to test the bottled beers. My friend Peter Eichhorn led this tasting; I was intentionally absent, since I wanted my opinion to be totally independent from Team B. I didn't share my results with them beforehand, either. In the case of Brigade B, the tasting was much more like a wine tasting since they didn't drink out of beer steins, but rather beer sommelier glasses. They are half-liter glasses that look like a mixture between a classic tulip glass and the Aventinus wheat beer glass made by G. Schneider & Sohn GmbH, and are suited

to tasting any kind of beer. By the way: even though the difference between the regular and the Oktoberfest Augustiner is hardly noticeable and thus factored into the assessment, this is in no way meant as a degradation of the regular "green" Augustiner beer, but should rather express that an Oktoberfest beer should stand out from the beer that is available all year. Like us, Brigade B had lots of fun during their tasting, however they were missing the sounds, smells, and visual charms of the beer tent. But you can't have it all, right?

Beer is a very special drink.

1ˢᵗ Place: Hacker-Pschorr: Nut brown with a reddish cast. Sturdy, coarse foam. This beer has more flavor than most of the others. More volume and malt sweetness. It is accompanied by a pleasantly roasted taste and smoky notes.

2ⁿᵈ Place: Hofbräu: The solid foam lasts a long time. The nose has a hint of carrot. The taste starts out pleasantly rich and impresses with an intense note of hops.

3ʳᵈ Place: Spaten: The solid foam comes away from the glass nicely. Malty and grainy notes. Some pepper and straw. A clean finish accompanied by a toasted flavor. Long aftertaste.

4ᵗʰ Place: Augustiner: Intense perlage. The nose is of vegetable brother and celery. The aroma remains pleasantly constant. The initial aromas are still just as noticeable in the finish. The difference between this beer and regular Augustiner is hardly noticeable.

5ᵗʰ Place: Löwenbräu: Very light. The coarse foam disappears quickly, too quickly. A light sourness accompanies the beer and makes it seem more like a Pils than an Oktoberfest beer.

6ᵗʰ Place: Paulaner: Grains and green apple in the nose. Brief bubbling, then the crispness and the foam are gone. Somewhat uninspired.

Summary of the Conclusions of Both Brigades

It's interesting that first, second, and fifth place were identical. This rating should not be used as a standard for the general quality of each of the types of beer, since all of the Oktoberfest beers vary from year to year. You can also have good or bad luck with a particular stein. It is clear that each beer at Oktoberfest gives its best. After all, they come from Munich.

Tip from an Expert
What is Strategic Drinking?

You should empty your stein slowly, but without dawdling. If you're thirsty, it can go a bit faster. But you shouldn't be careless when drinking Oktoberfest beer. Everyone should test their own tolerance before their Oktoberfest visit and set a drink limit before entering the tent. If you know how many glasses you can tolerate and how long you want to stay in the tent, you can easily calculate how frequently you need to order, and nothing stands in the way of your nice Oktoberfest visit.

Attention: All Oktoberfest beers (see above) are more flavorful and, above all, stronger than normal beer. A stein of Oktoberfest beer with an average of 6 percent alcohol content equals about eight servings of schnapps, according to the report on health and environment for the state capital of Munich. That should be taken into consideration during drink planning.

Oktoberfest goers during a forgotten historical moment.

"Carousing in the inns will not be tolerated at all from 6 to 11 in the morning, and only in the afternoons as long as it is not excessive. If excesses occur, the inn will be emptied by force and the guests are in danger of arrest."

Decree of the Munich Chief of Police, 1844

Number and frequency of drinks are not the only elements of strategic drinking. There are a few other variables which must be accounted for with increasing intoxication.

When, for example, you notice that you are in danger of crossing your drink limit (and with it your own limits), it is a good idea to take a bathroom break and secretly buy a mineral water from the food stand outside each beer tent (and drink it right on the spot), so that your visit doesn't go off course too quickly. This way, you are saved the pointed remarks of your neighbors at the table ("Why are you drinking water when there's beer?") and you can last longer. Whether it's two or four waters that gain you an extra beer (not counted in your beer limit) is a personal decision—one that you should make before you enter the tent.

Drunkenness is a great thing if you can handle it. It should progress harmoniously, including a timely finale. Trust the intoxication to tell you when it can't be increased any more. However, it sometimes delays that moment for a long time, since intoxication enjoys itself. I would say that intoxication can be split into three categories:

Tipsy: You're a bit silly but still clearly in control.

Buzzed: You're high-spirited and cheerful, and your inhibitions are lowered.

Sloshed: You're thoroughly drunk.

All three stages have their pros and cons. To be able to enjoy your nice visit to the beer tent, I recommend strategic drinking. When you reach the drink limit that you decided on beforehand, you should stop. You should also stop if you realize that you set your limit too high. If you're seeing the person sitting across from you twice and you can  only get up from the bench with your neighbor's help, you've long since passed your limit and that rarely ends well. It is good to combine strategic drinking with eating a lot. That's the best method. And just to be safe, try to ride the carousel before you're sloshed.

One does not wander unpunished among Bavarian beer steins.
Ferdinand August Bebel (1840–1913)

Even though there are stands selling spirits on Schaustellerstraße, and many offer high alcohol content, I recommend against mixing. The beer is potent enough. If you are particularly craving schnapps, keep it small.

Returning Your Drink: The Call of Nature and the Urinal

There are large urinals for the gentlemen between the tents as well as inside most of the large tents. For first-time Oktoberfest visitors, the men's urinals take some getting used to, since for reasons of space, everyone stands in the same room and answers the call of nature against a vertical surface. After his first visit to the urinals, a friend of mine from Hesse said, appalled, "that's beyond degrading!" It isn't though; we Bavarians are an earthy people, and you shouldn't be so small-minded. Plus, it has its advantages: men don't have to wait in line for long, and so the stream can flow as nature dictates. On one end, those who need to go urgently enter, inside there's room for everyone, and on the other end you leave feeling lighter and freer.

Why are the lines for the women's toilets always much longer than for the men's? For one, they don't have urinals, and for another, women simply have it harder, since many ladies use the moment of peace in the bathroom to send a text message, fix their makeup, or to think about things. Maybe some even take a little nap? Who knows? The lines are so long because women need three times as long for all that extra nonsense. And so, a request for all the ladies: use the toilet for what it was made for, wash your hands, and get out. Then there's room for the next in line and the unbelievable lines may come to an end. Anyway, you should plan extra time into your bathroom visit, since the path from your table to the toilet is usually longer than you think, and you often run into a friend or meet a new one. Everything takes time.

Some people prefer to answer the call outside in nature, but that is not allowed and will be punished with a fine. If

Next page: *See the painting* The Land of Cockaigne
by Pieter Brueghel the Elder

Make the best of your relief.

you find yourself on Schaustellerstraße or Wirtsbuden-straße and you have to go, friendly little angels point the way with their bows and arrows.

Tip from an Expert
The Parade of Tent Hosts or a Seat at the Tap?

On the first Saturday of Oktobefest is the traditional Parade of Tent Hosts into the Theresienwiese followed by the tapping of the first keg of beer. You have to decide: you can either see the Parade of Tent Hosts with their brewery horses and festively decorated wagons or you can grab a good seat in the tent or beer garden for the first keg. You can't do both.

Stopover

Where can I lay down for a little bit between two beer steins? In the western part of Oktoberfest, behind the beer tents, there's a gently sloping field where you can rest comfortably. But make sure that your valuables can't be snatched by strangers. It's also a good idea to look and see if the spot you'd like to lay down in is already occupied by one or several people. This field is popular with couples. Occasionally there are also visitors who don't feel well. To prevent unpleasant situations, you should not lie down right next to these people.

The Parade of Tent Hosts and Breweries is without a doubt a good show—and definitely worth a visit. All sorts of horse-drawn carts make their way through the cheering crowd to their tent, accompanied by tubas and oboes. It all starts a bit before eleven o'clock in the morning on Josephspitalstraße near the Sendlinger Gate, then the parade turns onto Sonnenstraße, and then left

I would be—grant me this request—the third in your band!
Friedrich Schiller (1759–1805)

onto Schwanthalerstraße. From there it continues to the Bavariaring and straight into Wirtsbudenstraße and to the assigned spots.

Since 1887, the march is a solid part of the Oktoberfest tradition. The first occurred a few years previously, in 1879, when the Styrian Hansä (master butcher, proprietor of an inn on Tegernseer Landstraße in Munich, and

"Bavarian Hercules") drove to the Theresienwiese with many guests, two coaches, and lots of fuss. However, he was stopped by guards and had to pay a hefty fine of one hundred marks—but that didn't stop him from getting a permit for it the next year and with that, beginning a lovely tradition.

Today the parade is led by the Münchner Kindl, followed directly by the current mayor of Munich. If you want to cheer on the hosts and their entourages, you should find a good spot in the crowd, preferably not behind two seven-foot giants. It's best to stand near the beer tent that you want to visit later, mixing fun with practicality.

If you decide against the parade and would rather get a seat near the tap, you should wake up early, since the seats are very sought-after, and you should know which tent you'd like to be in. If you want to see the mayor tap the first keg, you have to go to the Schottenhamel tent. It's very hard to find a seat here, since so many people want to see how many strikes with a big hammer it takes the master of ceremonies to tap the 200 liter beer keg (which has a lifespan of about 11 minutes at Oktoberfest).

The Münchner Kindl

The Münchner Kindl or "Munich Child" is the figure on the official crest of the Bavarian state capital. It is portrayed on a silver shield as a monk with a back cowl with a gold border and red shoes. He is looking to the right. In his left hand he is holding a red Bible, and his right hand is raised in blessing. You can see the Münchner Kindl in many spots around the city, such as on  manhole covers and tram cars, but also on souvenirs and postcards. Sometimes he looks really childlike, and sometimes in modern illustrations he is holding a radish or beer stein instead of a Bible. In old images he's shown in his original form of a monk, and can be kind of creepy (for example, on Gebsattel Bridge).

Usually it only takes a few strikes, since he's known for a long time what has to be done on the first Saturday of Oktoberfest. He doesn't want to look bad, so he surely practices in secret. The Bavarian Prime Minister may indulge in the first stein of beer while the mayor calls out the famous words "Ozapft is!" Then the rest of the Oktoberfest visitors can have a taste of the beer. It's very difficult to get into the tapping ceremony, or even get a seat in the Schottenhamel tent, and there aren't even any tricks. Except, perhaps, if you write an Oktoberfest handbook. That could work. Or so I've heard.

But for the most part, all the doors are packed and you can't get in, but there's no need to be sad. At twelve on the dot the hosts of each tent tap their first keg. This is accompanied by a traditional twelve gun salute, since it's twelve o'clock, anyway. Usually you have to wait a bit to get your first glass, since everyone wants one.

As is generally true at Oktoberfest, it is a good idea to arrive for the tapping early and in a small group, so that tiring table-searches and problems with entry mostly disappear. The best way to visit Oktoberfest is as a pair. That's how you have the best chance of being let in and finding a good seat. It's also wise to reserve a table early so you can't go wrong. But by the time of the tapping, the quota will have long been filled. More importantly, on the day of the

tapping, you should know if your desired tent is on the east or west side of the road. Due to the Parade of Tent Hosts, you will get stuck on one side of the road. You should plan ahead strategically so that you don't have to walk far out of the way. If you want to be in the Armbrustschützen tent, Hacker tent, Hofbräu tent, Hippo-drom, the Schottenhamel tent, or the Winzerer Fähndl (so, in a tent on the west side of Wirtsbudenstraße), you should get off the train at Schwanthalerhöhe or Hackerbrücke and enter from the west or "behind," over the field. If you want to be in the Löwenbräu tent, the Pschorr-Bräurosl tent, the Augustiner-Festhalle, Fischer-Vroni, the Ammer, or the Ochsenbraterei, you can get off at the Theresienwiese and let the current lead you.

Be embraced, you millions!

Traditional Cuisine—Food

Wiesnhendl—Roast Chicken

If you amble down the paths between the tents, vehicles, and booths, you'll pass countless stands offering fish rolls, radishes, cheese squares, schnitzel rolls, roast nuts, candied fruit, cotton candy, and other tasty treats. And when you get to the beer tent, if not sooner, you'll have your choice of cold and warm dishes. You can head to Oktoberfest without eating anything beforehand, confident that you'll find something when you get there. It's just important that you bring enough cash, because otherwise you're faced with the question of chicken or beer. You can't have one without the other, since beer goes so well with chicken and chicken goes so well with beer that you shouldn't abstain from either. Plus, you need a little bit of support when you're drinking Oktoberfest beer.

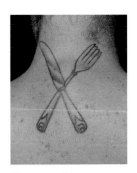

They say this arrangement means "I want seconds!"

After beer and big pretzels, half a roast chicken is the Oktoberfest classic. A half chicken costs a bit more

A discount for 46-year-olds or for people born in 1946?

than a stein of beer, but it's nearly as much fun. Why do chickens taste better at Oktoberfest than anywhere else? Because they are prepared with the highest quality ingredients, seasoned with a sophisticated mix of spices, stuffed with fresh parsley, and spread with hand-churned butter. Many of the chickens come from organic farms where they're feed high-quality feed and get to be three times as old as their comrades at "regular" farms. They say that organic chicken is more tender. But one thing is certain: all the roast chicken at Oktoberfest is delicious, with crispy skin and juicy meat. Not to mention spread with good, Bavarian butter. Sometimes you get an old-fashioned moist towelette with your chicken that smells of artificial lemon and helps you clean your fingers. The scent is fake, but somehow it's a part of the experience. If they aren't giving out towelettes, you can politely ask for one. By the way, it's completely acceptable to eat your chicken with your hands—no matter what Miss Manners would have to say about that. A knife and fork works just as well, but it's the boring method for the faint of heart. As boys we tossed the hot pieces of chicken into each other's mouths. When I tried to continue this lovely tradition with a girlfriend a few years later, she just didn't get it.

Fischsemmel and Ochsensemmel—Fish and Beef Rolls

Fish rolls have long been a part of the experience, too. A traditional fish roll is topped with herring, pickles, and onions. The juicy herring soaks into the roll and makes it soft. Because of the many onions and the fish smell, it is not a good idea to eat a fish roll right before kissing someone.

Once, I met a young lady in the Hacker tent and before long, we were smooching. Then we went for a walk around the fairgrounds. She was suddenly hungry. She said, "Let's each get a fish roll. If we both eat onions, we can keep kissing, because neither of us will notice." My answer: "Let's eat some candied fruit instead. There's a lower risk." Between the Augustiner tent and the Pschorr-Bräurosl tent, on the south side of the Augustiner tent near Wirtsbudenstraße, there is a stand with a

One must wait until digestion to say anything about the wonderful city of Munich. Franz Kafka (1883–1924)

charmingly priced selection of fish rolls: Fisch Hellberg, from Erlangen. They have salted herring in sherry sauce, river crab rolls with honey mustard sauce (drippy, but delicious), salmon, calamari, beer-batter fried fish, and trout—everything a hungry stomach demands. The rolls are baked fresh on location and are some of the crispiest at Oktoberfest. I must recommend them!

There are many stands selling beef at Oktoberfest. Each cook has his own special sauce and guards his secret recipe more strictly than the CIA. A beef roll is a good thing to tide you over during your visit to Oktoberfest. They all taste good; you can't really go wrong with any of them.

Since people generally stay on the fairgrounds for several hours, I recommend enjoying your beef roll before visiting the beer tent. That way you'll at least have something delicious to tide you over, and you'll feel strengthened by the hearty beef. The beef rolls at Kalbs-Kuchl are legendary: the beef is fresh, the vegetables are crisp, and the special sauce truly is special. Also, logically, delicious: the fine beef rolls in the Ochsenbraterei, where you can read the name and weight of the animal that you are currently enjoying on a big sign.

Brezn—Pretzels

Oktoberfest pretzels are distinctive in that they are about four or five times as big as regular pretzels. They also have a perfectly balanced relationship between the outer

Look, Ma, no hands!

The three traditional pretzel bakers at Oktoberfest are:
- ● Brezn Piller from Karlsfeld
- ● Bäckerei Ziegler from Munich
- ● Bäckerei Ratschiller from Holzkirchen

crispiness and the inner softness. Like their smaller cousins, they are made from yeast, salt, flour, water, and butter or margarine. The only difference is that, because they are so beloved, they are often sold out just a few minutes after they're prepared, and so pretzels at Oktoberfest are always fresh. You should eat them quickly after buying them, because they can get soggy due to the humidity in the beer tents. Pretzels belong at Oktoberfest just like beer. I'm of the opinion that you should buy your pretzels at Oktoberfest itself, and not beforehand at a stand on Hackerbrücke or at some discount shop to save money. Everyone has to decide for themselves. If I'm traveling to Italy, I'm not going to buy a bottle of Chianti Classico at the supermarket before I go. Capisce?

The pretzels at Oktoberfest are mostly very good and you can see if they're no longer fresh or if they were baked for too long. It does take a trained eye, but you'll develop that over time. And please, take note: an Oktoberfest pretzel is not to be eaten alone. It should be shared.

Kas—Cheese

In addition to beer, cheese also goes well with pretzels. It's best as a snack, cut into cubes and sprinkled with pepper and salt. Both vegetarians and meat eaters can enjoy it. And if you arrive back late to your group from a bathroom trip or a ride on the Ferris wheel, you'll get a joyful greeting if you bring along a nice plate of emmentaler or gouda.

Remedies and Supplements

If you're like me and you go to Oktoberfest often, you'll need a little bit of help (no later than the first week) to make it through two weeks of Oktoberfest healthy and lively. Otherwise, you may look pretty haggard after a few

Don't try. Charles Bukowski (1920–1994)

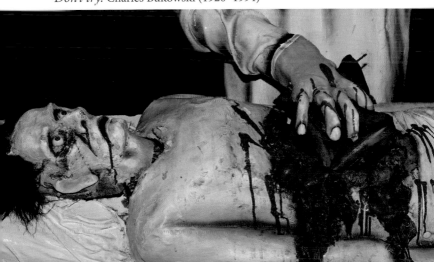

days, dragging yourself from tent to tent. And nobody needs that nonsense. So here are a few valuable tips:

1. Milk Thistle: Milk thistle is a plant with large, jagged green/white marbled leaves. It protects and strengthens your liver, detoxifies, stimulates bile flow. The preparation I recommend is called Ardeyhepan. It protects the liver from damage, stabilizes the membranes of liver cells, and absorbs toxins before they reach  the liver. This way, new liver cells can grow. My personal recommendation: two tablets in the morning before your visit, and one when you get home.

2. Artichoke: Artichoke lowers cholesterol and stimulates metabolic processes between your liver and gallbladder. The preparation I prefer is called Ardeycholan. It increases bile production, lowers the production of cholesterol in the liver cells, and supports the breakdown of dietary fat, the elimination of waste, and the absorption of fat-soluble vitamins. Here I have the same advice: two tablets before your visit, one after.

3. Mineral Nutrients: It's best to get minerals in their natural form, preferably from low-carbonation mineral water. Approximately three 24-oz bottles per day is perfect. Even if it sounds ridiculous, since you're drinking liters of beer, it's important for your body to get enough water. It will thank you. I recommend St. Primus Heilwasser from Adelholzener. Drink nice and slowly. It won't kill you.

The Tents

All about the Tents

For many Oktoberfest goers, the beer tent is, understandably, the most important part of their visit. Here's where you socialize, make deals, propose to your partner, gossip, dance, dress up, eat, drink, and sing. Here's where you tease and flirt, slander and exclude, love and trust, and desire and regret. In short: the beer tent is where you'll find real life.

A strong woman—17 at once!

Each side of each tent faces a particular cardinal direction, so the four entrances to each tent are named accordingly, for convenience. You can simplify meetings by meeting at one of the labeled doors. The southern entrances are labeled "S," the western entrances "W," the eastern entrances "O," and the northern entrances "N." Even this can be confusing when intoxicated, but generally entrance "S2," for example, is pretty easy to find.

Good to know: Near the main and side entrances of the large beer tents there are over a hundred "bread ladies." Aside from giant pretzels, they also sell rolls, pretzel sticks, beer pretzels, and other baked goods that go well with beer. By the outside walls and in front of the tent entrances there are 44 booths and 72 stalls where you can get snacks, non-alcoholic drinks, tobacco products, wurst, cheese, fruit, deli food, sweets, and many nice souvenirs. You can also find Charivari pendants, collectors' edition beer steins, card games, hat feathers, hats, t-shirts with slogans that are funny (or are supposed to be funny), pins, bandanas, and other useful items to buy for yourself or as a gift. And, of course, the famous gingerbread hearts.

In the tents, it's always lively and crowded. If possible, you should reserve your table early—no later than March. If you don't have a reservation, you should try to go on weekdays before 3:00 p.m. or on Sunday evenings.

My heart is in my dirndl.

Hearts in our Hearts

Lebkuchen (gingerbread) hearts are a traditional part of Oktoberfest. They offer something for everyone. Lovers can "subtly" share lovely, intimate expressions ("my little sparrow," "I love you," "pookie," "hottie," "love fairy," "stud," "Oktoberfest babe," "hawk," or "naughty gnome"). Anyone can say what needs to be said ("beer please," "not picky," "I'll eat anything," "kiss me," "drunk as a skunk").

Wonderful. Try to avoid buying gingerbread hearts that make use of apostrophes, because few people have mastered proper use of apostrophes. If you are buying a heart for a crush,  make sure not to be too clever, since that can easily go wrong. It's better to choose a small, charming heart with something nice on it, like "sweetie." You can't go wrong and everyone wins.

The tents are packed at every other time, and you will be hard-pressed to find a seat. This is especially true for families. By the way, there are no children under the age of six allowed in the tents after 8:00 p.m. Even with parental supervision. The lawmakers said so, and for once they thought of something sensible.

Apostrophes: Many presenters and salespeople want their signs, menus, and marquees to be in particularly flashy Bavarian. To do so, they use apostrophes to violently contract German words to resemble the Bavarian dialect, and the results are mostly grammatically absurd. I've even seen some simply stick an apostrophe into a word at random: "Lies'l," "schmeck't," "Wirt'sleut," or "Leberka's."

Closing time in the regular beer tents is 11:00 p.m., so last call is promptly at 10:30. In the food halls and coffee tents, the bar closes at 11:00 p.m. The party only goes on for two more hours in the wine tent and the Käfer Wies'n-Schänke. But remember: after last call, finish your drinks as quickly as possible because working the tents is hard and all the servers are looking forward to relaxing. Even they have to rest sometime. So don't beg and plead; when it's closed, it's closed, basta. Tomorrow is another day and there will always be another Oktoberfest.

It's all gone, and it's a shame.

Music in the Beer Tent

One distinctive feature of the music in the beer tents is the so-called "Wiesn Hit." There's one almost every year. One can't say exactly when you know if there is one, or what it is. Sometimes it takes until well into the second week before we see who wins the race. On the other hand, sometimes it happens so unusually quickly that you don't even notice at first. When everyone begins making the same gestures and singing the same song out of nowhere, there's a good chance that you're hearing this year's Wiesn Hit. But if that happens on the first day, it could be that you're hearing last year's hit. A Wiesn Hit comes with fame, accomplishment, and a decent royalty check

Take a walk on the wild side.

that turns out to be much less than it first seems like. You wouldn't be set for life, but you get something, of course. But you'd be fooling yourself if you think you'll get international fame, a bathtub full of champagne, and regular dinners with Prince Charles, Giselle Bündchen, and Robbie Williams. Many musicians and lyricists still try desperately to write a Wiesn Hit, but very few succeed. There aren't any musical or lyrical rules to follow. It's partly a matter of current tastes, the feelings of the Oktoberfest bandmaster, and the political situation. Sometimes you can tell beforehand which songs have the potential of becoming Wiesn Hits by what's popular in the nightlife like at El Arena or Après-ski bars. Chris Boettcher, a dear friend of mine, landed the Wiesn Hit in 2009 with the satirical song "Zehn Meter geh." It by no means made him rich, but he was still happy that his song had achieved such an honorable distinction. And it's a very good song.

Many dream their whole lives of writing the next Wiesn Hit, but for some it would be enough just to conduct an Oktoberfest band once. The musicians have long since realized that, and are happy to make a deal in exchange for a generous donation. You often see people from the crowd clowning around in front of the band, conducting "Country Roads" or "Joanna." You have to gauge according to your own self-confidence and limits whether you'd put on a good show or whether you'd be the only one who thought it wasn't embarrassing. My tip: put those hundred euros into beer, instead.

Tip from an Expert

How Do You Get into the Tent When It's Full? And Where Do You Sit When You're in, but Don't Have a Reserved Seat?

When it's really crowded—all day on the weekend and weekdays after 3:00 p.m.—you shouldn't go to Oktoberfest in a group of more than two people without a reservation, since you may not be let into the beer garden even if the weather is nice. If you can't or won't follow this basic advice, don't despair, because where there's a will, there's a way.

When you are standing before closed beer tent doors, one thing is always a good idea: always be friendly, and sometimes security will let you in. If they are being strict, you should respect that, because there is always a valid reason. They have to watch out for safety in the tent.

Even the smallest cottage has room.

No one likes to turn away a guest, so it's never a matter of negative feelings, just safety precautions.

A small tip: if you know someone in the tent and he can come over and convincingly prove to security that there is room at his table, you may potentially be let in. This process certainly requires a lot of charm.

If the doors won't open, persistence helps along with friendliness. Either you wait long enough in front of a strategically promising (not mobbed) entrance, or you go around and around the tent until opportunity presents itself. Seeing the doors open is a good sign that something good might happen. If you don't get a chance, you can always go to a smaller tent for a while or try again to get a spot in the beer garden.

If none of that works, there's still one very promising tactic: in many tents, wristbands are given out with a reservation that allow automatic entrance to the tent. Simply ask people with reservations who are waiting to be let in if everyone in their party is there. If not, there have to be extra wristbands that you could potentially buy from them. This method works very well and is totally legitimate.

The best secret tip I can give you for getting into the tent is this: get there early or make a reservation. It's like Christmas shopping: Oktoberfest comes every year and you have plenty of time to get informed and make sure you get a reservation.

If you've made it into the tent without a reservation and can't find a seat, you should ask a server or security guard where the unreserved area is. As a rule, you will find a niche (as a pair) before long.

The beer tables at Oktoberfest are almost always standard beer garden tables with room for ten average-sized people. For example, if ten Top Models are sitting at the

Where Should I Go with Serious Work Colleagues?

If you find yourself at Oktoberfest on business with colleagues to whom you don't want to bear your soul, it's best to go to a "serious" tent like the Armbrustschützen tent, the Ammer, or one of the small, "dignified" tents like Poschner's. Alternatively, if it's a nice afternoon, you can sit in one of the many lovely beer gardens in front of the tents. It's always nice there, you can have a little something to eat, and it's right in the middle of Oktoberfest. Guard against  possible derailment by drinking no more than two steins and promptly and politely taking your leave from your dear colleagues. Then you're free to head into a tent on your own time and let your hair down.

table, there's sure to be room for two more slender men. But if ten full-bodied head chefs are sitting there, those two guys would be falling off their seats. You must ask with manners and understanding. Don't be shy!

Some people hold seats for their friends for hours. That's not okay, and in these cases you might offer to hold the seat for them. If the friends arrive after that, it's only fair to stand up and let them have the seat. In Bavaria, your word and your handshake are like a written contract. It's tradition.

Life in the beer tents is very fast paced. Unexpected tables often free up when a group decides to seek their fortunes elsewhere. That's when you have to act quickly!

The Big Tents

It's more crowded and louder in the big tents than in the little tents. Even though the little tents have plenty to offer (and I'll go into detail later), the baseline mood in the big tents is generally more euphoric. And with that, the flirtation factor goes up, too. There's always a lot to see, since

people are eating, drinking, kissing, laughing, and celebrating. There are stein-laden servers, hosts, sour pickle sellers, pretzel sellers, radish sellers, photographers, and souvenir sellers with trays going in and out the doors. It smells of boiled and roasted food and beer and there's always a pulsating blanket of sound. And everyone is happy.

In the beer gardens you are allowed to smoke and to bring food. Only drinks need to be ordered there. And they don't let you get away with bringing in drinks. It makes sense, but not everyone gets it. So I'm writing it one more time as a precaution.

By the way, there are only six types of beer at Oktoberfest because there are only six purely Munich-based breweries. Oktoberfest should stay a Munich event. And I think it's perfect the way it is and it doesn't need to get any bigger. I can get a Tegernseer Helle or King Ludwig beer the rest of the year.

There are seven brewery tents: Augustiner Festhalle (Augustiner), Festhalle Pschorr-Bräurosl (Hacker-Pschorr), Hacker-Festzelt (Hacker-Pschorr), Hofbräu-Festzelt (Hofbräu), Löwenbräu Festzelt (Löwenbräu), Ochsenbraterei (Spaten), and Winzerer Fähndl (Paulaner). And there are seven Host's tents: Armbrustschützen (Paulaner), Fischer-Vroni (Augustiner), Festhalle Schottenhamel (Spaten), Hippodrom (Spaten), Käfer Wics'n-Schänke (Paulaner), Schützen-Festzelt (Löwenbräu), and Weinzelt (in addition to wine, they serve Paulaner weiss beer).

My first time in the beer tents was with my grandparents at the tender age of nine. My grandmother was intent on my grandfather not drinking beer, and she dragged us back out quickly. My grandfather was very interested in technical things, and he started critiquing the construction of the tents, which in his eyes was "botched up crap," as he loudly announced. He was probably just annoyed that he hadn't gotten a beer and wanted to vent his frustration.

The older I got, the more the beer tent became a part of my heart. I began to feel at home. Unfortunately, my mailman still refuses to bring my mail to the beer tent during Oktoberfest. But I'm still working on him. Maybe one day I'll convince him. It's one of my great goals in life.

"Now let's put it to the test."

Hacker-Festzelt
Bavarian Heavens

The Hacker tent has been at Okto-
berfest since 1907. They obviously
serve Hacker-Pschorr beer here. The mostly young drinkers are largely from Bavaria, the mood is boisterous, people stand on the benches, the flirtation factor is high, and
you can really let go. The Hacker tent has a real atmosphere
and fills up rapidly.

Important Information

The ceiling of a beer tent as seen from inside the tent
is colloquially known as "the heavens." And the heaven
of the Hacker tent is particularly beautiful. Like the
Bavarian flag, it's blue and white and is decorated with
clouds and stars. The ceiling in the Hacker tent is rightfully called the Bavarian Heavens. So that visitors can
see the heavens over Bavaria as closely as possible, the
back of the ceiling can be opened in nice weather. Guests
sit under the free blue and white heavens—the Bavarian
Heavens.

A secret power makes sure that the hearts in this tent
beat particularly hard. You get closer and everything
is filled with a magical lightness. Is it the decorations?
The good mood? The music? The beer? The clouds? The
wonderful servers? The extremely friendly host, Toni
Roiderer? It's probably a mixture of many things. Once,
I saw two young guys, clearly divided over choice of beer

tent, fighting in front of the Hacker tent in their lovely Upper Palatinate accents. Two young women who had been watching the scene for a while were very amused and they smoothed things over. The four sat down in the beer garden next to our table. A few hours later, one of the guys went off with pink cheeks and a blissful expression, hand in hand with the blonde. The other was getting very familiar with the brunette.

On the last night of Oktoberfest it is particularly romantic in this tent. As a grand finale, countless sparklers twinkle among the crowd under the Bavarian Heavens, the band sings "Sierra Madre," and everyone holds each other and comforts themselves with the thought that the next Oktoberfest will eventually come!

Inner Life

The inside of the Hacker tent has room for about 6,900 people. The servers are lively and gallant, but not always free to chat due to their large work load. But that's okay, the important thing is that the beer comes fast. If you do have to wait a bit for your beer, it's a lovely place to let your gaze wander. The scenery was beautifully redesigned in 2004 by legendary movie set designer Rolf Zehetbauer (known for *Das Boot*, *Ödipussi*, *Space Patrol Orion*, and *Cabaret*, among others), decorated by the great painter Rudolf Reinstadler with historical buildings, beautiful landscapes, scenes of Munich daily life, and Bavarian snapshots. If you're not sitting in one, you can look at the various theme boxes. They're called Karl Valentin, Liesl Karlstadt, Karussell, Wirtshaus, or Biergarten. And your beer will arrive before you know it.

Music

Up on the music pavilion are Schäffler folk dancers with their big wreaths who dance for sixteen days. Below, the excited crowd dances. The band is on a rotating platform so that all the guests can see the musicians from a good angle without getting up. And the musicians can see all the guests without moving.

Between 7:00 and 10:45 p.m. there's no stopping. For years that's been when the cult band Cagey Strings from

Tip: the fresh tartare is to die for.

Munich really gets the audience pumped up. Aside from the Wiesn Hits, they play music that is a bit unusual for Oktoberfest, from indie rock to AC/DC to oldies. The audience often sings along with the humorous refrains. The rest of the time "Die Kirchdorfer" give it their all, and the visitors to the Hacker tent are already standing on the benches by the afternoon, when everyone else is still sleeping off yesterday's hangover.

Food and Drink

Good Hacker-Pschorr is on tap, along with non-alcoholic drinks. But here it is: the kitchen in the Hacker tent is amazing. It belongs to none other than Oktoberfest legend Toni Roiderer. He always has a great selection of specialties "in petto": beef, suckling pig, various wurst, and of course juicy, finely spiced roast chicken. Toni Roiderer is not only a master butcher and host of Wildpark Straßlach and, since 1989, of the Hacker tent, he's also the spokesperson for the tent hosts.

There's a rumor that Toni Roiderer was once not let into his own tent. He introduced himself politely, but the security guards said, "Anyone could say that." Since then all the workers have apparently been given photos of the members of the Roiderer family.

Beer Garden

The outside area around the Hacker tent has around 2,400 seats and is a great place for meetings and social interactions in both good and bad weather. The organization is excellent and the mood is high-spirited. The servers are quick and very friendly, and leaving them a decent tip is important. I have five favorite servers in the Hacker beer garden: Bianca, Barbara, Andrea, Silvia, and Sepp. Please treat them well, it won't hurt you. Once I was with seven friends in the Hacker beer garden on a bustling Oktoberfest day. We got in just before the guards closed the whole tent. Inside, it looked as though the eight of us would never find seats together; all the tables were full. Bianca reassured us and said she would take care of it. She went right to work, asked a few smaller groups to move around, and within a few minutes we had a whole table to ourselves.

Seats: 9,300
Mood: Party
Family Friendly: in the beer garden or very early in the day
Flirtation Factor: extremely high
Beer: Hacker-Pschorr
Host: Toni Roiderer
Reservatioins: www.hacker-festzelt.de

Augustiner Festhalle
Tradition and Munich Togetherness

In the Augustiner tent, they serve— wait for it—Augustiner. Since the Bavarian people particularly love this beer, you always meet a lot of natives in this tent. The mood in both the tent and beer garden is dignified, and there are visitors of all ages. The Augustiner tent has been part of Oktoberfest since 1898 and is a rather peaceful, nice, and friendly tent. It might be the homiest tent at Oktoberfest.

Important Infortmation

Traditionally, the Augustiner Brewery has avoided advertising in public space and is the only Munich brewery to still use old-fashioned bottles. They are traditional brown German beer bottles in which beer and lemon soda were sold until the 1990s. Additionally, Augustiner is the only brewery that serves its beer from wooden kegs at Oktoberfest, called "stags" (capacity: 200 liters). The Augustiner beer is an Oktoberfest beer, but it is called "Edelstoff" like the year-round export beer. You can marvel at the Edelstoff kegs in front of the tent, and they also make a good meeting place. But make sure you clarify in advance whether when you say "the left keg" you mean the left when entering the tent or the left when exiting the tent, otherwise your whole plan will fall apart, especially if you've already had a little beer.

Inner Life

There is room for 6,000 people inside the Augustiner tent. It has a Munich atmosphere, the music is reserved, and the mood is comfortable and cozy in the more Bavarian sense: live and let live. If you can't find a free table and you ask nicely, you'll definitely find someone who will let you join their table before long. For those who don't speak Bavarian: this can happen in a few different ways.

 If you're alone, the natives might say "Sitz di her!" which basically means "Just come sit down." If you're with a group, the plural version of this offer is "Setzts eich her!" If you ask your new neighbor if he's sure that you can take one of these highly desired seats, the answer in the Augustiner tent might be "Basst scho!" ("It's ok"), "Geht si aus" ("Fine by me"), or "Wenns ned no mehra werds . . ." ("You are welcome to sit, as long as the number of members in your group doesn't increase"). The Munich way of speaking can seem snippy to outsiders, but it's meant with love.

Music

The Augustiner tent was the first to have its own band at the beginning of the twentieth century. At that time they also distributed lyrics sheets and sticks to keep the beat among the audience. These days the "Augustiner Fest-kapelle" plays daily under the leadership of Reinhardt Hagitte from early to late with the following recipe: brass band music all day, dance music at night. The music has an old Munich flair appropriate for a traditional beer tent: friendly, upbeat, and pleasant. Good for swaying to. Good for gossiping, as well.

Food and Drink

In the Augustiner tent they serve Augustiner Edelstoff. It's strong and drinkable and shouldn't be underestimated. After the third stein, many have had trouble finding their own seat. The food is good; there's a lunch menu that changes daily with something for everyone: many traditional dishes such as the very juicy roast chicken, the wonderful meat plate, or a crispy pork knuckle—and all for a fair price.

Beer Garden

In the outside area of the Augustiner tent, there is room for 2,500 people. With some patience, you'll find a seat, and conversations with natives are not far behind. You can learn a lot there. For example, my friend and colleague Michi Dietmayr once explained to a visitor from the nearby countryside that Munich residents call Munich "München" and not "Minga." You can hear about this experience in his song, "Kaschbal."

The servers in the beer garden are speedy and sometimes a bit grumpy, which in Bavaria is more of a seal of authenticity than a shortcoming. The mood in the outside area is often more raucous than inside, but not always. You should walk around before deciding where you want to sit.

Seats: 8,500
Mood: Traditional old Munich
Family Friendly: Yes
Flirtation Factor: It can be done
Beer: Augustiner
Host: Manfred Vollmer
Reservations: www.festhalle-augustiner.com

Armbrustschützenzelt
Huntsmen and the Good Old Days

Since 1935, the crossbow championship has been held in this tent, so the Armbrustschützen tent is beloved by hunting clubs and traditional groups. The tent arrangement accommodates the house shooting range. The shooters used to aim at wooden eagles, but today they use targets, which doesn't diminish the fun of shooting with a crossbow. A nice alternative to the "young" tents, here you can drink a beer in peace and hear old traditional music.

Important Information

The original incarnation of this tent first appeared in 1895, mainly for crossbow shooters. The legendary, funny, and affable host Richard Süßmeier made the tent what it is today. He is legendary for some truly funny tricks, like how he once stitched another half chicken onto a whole chicken, then demonstrated for the cameras how you could get three roasted half chickens out of one chicken. Every year he can be seen in the Augustiner cellar for the tapping, but he's also always liked to slip out in costume. He often likes to dress up as Napoleon Bonaparte. So his nickname, "The Napoleon of the Hosts," didn't exactly come from nowhere. And his responses to

questions are always quick and clever. According to legend, when a journalist asked him for the third time what an Oktoberfest tent host earned, he said "one on the right and one on the left."

Inner Life

There is room for 5,830 people inside the Armbrustschützen tent. You can see the band from almost every seat, and the mood is relaxed and good. The decorations are based on a militia group or a hunting lodge: there are shields and plaques everywhere with images of Bavarian hunting themes. Mrs. Inselkammer, the wife of tent host Peter Inselkammer, designed the beautiful themes of the boxes and painted the signs herself. The boxes are called hunter box, badger box, tracking box, or pheasant box. But you can take a seat even if you aren't a woodsman! There is a big wild boar enthroned above the doorway which is traditionally dressed up by workers and friends of the tent at the beginning of Oktoberfest. It's been seen as an alien, Santa Claus, and a silent film star. If you want to see it, you have to be quick, since when Oktoberfest business really begins on the morning of the tapping, the boar drops its masquerade.

The servers inside and outside are well trained, friendly, and busy as bees. There are no male servers in the Armbrustschützen tent. In the parterre are the older women, and in the balconies are the younger women. The young men can usually be found in the upper regions.

Music

It is a rotation of the "Platzl Oktoberfestkapelle Gerleigner" and the "Wolfsegger Buam." You'll hear good beer tent music, more for swaying to than for totally rocking out, since hunters keep their cool.

Food and Drink

There's cool Paulaner beer and countless woodsmen's delicacies like roast deer with Spätzle, but also traditional Oktoberfest dishes like grilled duck with red cabbage or tender roast veal. The host family Inselkammer offers a free Oktoberfest visit with food and drink to 200 senior citizens each year and donates a large amount for social projects in Munich.

Beer Garden

The outside area has space for 1,620 guests and is a cozy place where you can have a nice beer and forget your worldly troubles like stress and burnout. Here, tradition takes you in. You meet many Bavarians from the countryside, and people talk and joke in a dignified manner, a bit like at the Royal Municipal Court of Bavaria. No one would be surprised if the agricultural minister and his white beard came by.

Seats: 7,450
Mood: Country house
Family Friendly: Yes
Flirtation Factor: Low
Beer: Paulaner
Host: Peter Inselkammer
Reservations: www.armbrustschuetzenzelt.de

Festhalle Pschorr-Bräurosl
Hacker-Pschorr Beer and Joie de Vivre

"If there's nothing going on in the Bräu-rosl, that's your fault!" With its wonderful band, good beer, and relaxed atmosphere, the Bräurosl is the tent that can be most appropriately described as "sexy." First, Bräurosl, the symbol of the tent, is enticingly feminine and erotic. Then, there's the Alpine embodiment of every woman's dreams: the "Goaßlschnal-zer." Additionally, a huge party happens here on "Gay

---

Goaßlschnalzer

A "Goaßl" is a kind of whip originally used by carriage and coach drivers in Austria and Bavaria. The whip can be flicked in the air to made a loud crack. Back then, each driver had his own trademark whip crack to make himself stand out from the other drivers. Today, Goaßlschnalzer ("whip-snappers") are generally men in Tracht who crack their whips in time with the music in beer tents or at other events. It makes for an exciting show!

*Sunday." Two large maypoles stand in front of the entrance
as the symbols of the tent. For generations, the hosts have
come from the hospitable and likeable Heide family. Every
year, the friendly tent host Schorsch Heide takes a bow in
front of his tent. As he should.*

Important Information

The word "Bräurosl" has nothing to do with a rose or a
brewery horse, but was rather the pet name of the brewery family daughter, Rosi Pschorr. In 1901, the court
painter Karl Schultheis painted the first portrait of Bräurosl on the gable wall of the first Pschorr tent at Oktoberfest. And she was beautiful. Bavarian. Lively. A bright
bonnet on her head, a flowing dress, and a silk shawl on
her shoulders. Legend says she really existed, this beautiful daughter of master brewer Joseph Pschorr, and that
she refreshed herself every day with a good drink. At the
parade of tent hosts, you can still see her up on the brewery horse, a beer stein in her hand. Whether she is the
real Bräurosl or an actress, no one can be sure. But at any
rate, the Bräurosl tent was and is something very special . . .

The tent has its own yodeler during Oktoberfest, who
adds to the mood with traditional Bavarian song. To
honor Rosi Pschorr, she answers to the name Bräurosl
during Oktoberfest.

Inner Life

In 2004, the aisles were raised, which had an excellent effect on air circulation. The inside of the tent is kept intentionally simple, without paintings or colorful decorations. The people make it colorful! It's always very merry in this tent. It's hard to get in since it got around that things can really take off here and that "interpersonal" relationships can be easily made. Complete strangers often find themselves in each others' arms, as if guided by a magic hand. Sometimes they lose each other in the crowd, but it's okay, since they quickly find new, attractive people to kiss.

If you're lucky, you may meet the host, Schorsch Heide, who holds a beer stein with an elegant technique that's

Gay Sunday in the Bräurosl Tent

On the second day of Oktoberfest (the first Sunday), Bräurosl always appears on the stage at noon and calls out "Servus, Grüezi, und Hallo!" Then it really gets crazy in the tent, especially on the balcony, but for that you have to pay a cover price and make an early reservation. It's not for the weak, so be warned, but if you aren't a wallflower, you're guaranteed to have a ton of fun. Just between us: they really know how to party.

unique to him. And he's always ready for a nice conversation. Here, you can really throw yourself into pleasure, whether you're sitting in the middle, in the galleries, or in the boxes. The Bräurosl ensures a good mood and a good time.

Music

In the Bräurosl tent, the "Ludwig Thoma Musikantent" and the "Südtiroler Spitzbaum" switch off and make sure there's great, mixed musical entertainment. And in the evening, the Goaßlschnalzer show up and start cracking their whips. There's certainly something that anyone can appreciate.

Food and Drink

For very hungry people, there's the Bräurosl Food Plate, with veal knuckle, duck, suckling pig, potato dumplings, and red cabbage, but you can also order Leberkäs with gravy and potato salad or wurst salad. Everything is fresh and masterfully prepared. For early risers, there's lunch from 11:30 a.m. to 2:30 p.m., which changes daily.

And there's good Hacker-Pschorr beer to go with it. The double name Hacker-Pschorr comes from the marriage of Joseph Pschorr to the daughter of another brewery family, Maria Theresia Hacker, in 1793. With that, they merged the two breweries together. To honor both families, the newly founded brewery got both names. And the beer still enjoys great popularity today.

Beer Garden

The outside area of the Bräurosl tent is characterized by cheerfulness and joy for all ages. The servers are funny and cheeky, the beer is bubbly and golden, the aisles are full, and in general, everything is swinging. It's almost like a very big (2,500 seats) private garden party. You feel at home right away and get into conversations quickly. That's true for all of Oktoberfest, but here it's just a little more true. Perhaps it's because the spirit of the late tent host and spokesperson for the hosts, Willy Heide, watches over the guests and instills every visitor with his unshakeable happiness. And when it's hopping in the beer garden, you can only guess what it's like inside.

Seats: 8,500
Mood: Party, Party, Party!
Family Friendly: Not at all
Flirtation Factor: Tremendous
Beer: Hacker-Pschorr
Host: Schorsch and Renate Heide
Reservations: www.braeurosl.de

Hippodrom
Stars of the Circus Ring

The Hippodrom is right next to the main entrance. You also can't miss the bright colors. Red dominates the façade, with yellow tagging along, too. The name "Hippodrom" has nothing to do with being hip. The ancient Greek word "Hippodromo" means "horse racetrack." This name is appropriate, since for decades real horses were on show in a ring. These days it is mostly a meeting place for the prominent and upper class. Along with the Käfer Wies'n-Schänke, the Hippodrom has become one of the trendy tents due to its chic, glamorous, and Bavarian charm mixed with a lively party program and world-famous celebrities.

Important Information

The Hippodrom was the first tent to offer a schedule of entertainment along with its beer and food. Like a circus tent, the middle was a ring with a racetrack where the cheerful visitors tried to ride one of the 25 strong horses, which wasn't always easy after a few steins of Spaten beer. The racetrack existed until the 1980s. These days there are no more horses in the Hippodrom, but there are beautiful people and a mixture of Bavarian and international flair.

Inner Life

Inside, there is room for 3,300 people. Aside from the regular beer tables, there are smaller tables, standing tables, and an upper level gallery that wraps around the tent. At the champagne bar, many successful business deals are made and perhaps double as many love affairs are begun. Everything is well organized and you must reserve early, because the rules are strict. You have to break eggs to make an omelet, and it's first come, first served, so you have to get everything in order early and you won't be disappointed: here it's fun, there's a great atmosphere, and you might recognize some famous faces. Rudolph Moshammer sang here in his day (God rest his soul) and in 2006 Paris Hilton brought her champagne in a can, starting a scandal that resulted in a rule that no more advertisements could be filmed at Oktoberfest. Apparently, Paris refused to walk the distance between the entrance and the Hippodrom (perhaps 400 feet), and insisted on driving in her limo. Of course, that wasn't possible, and she was forced to stress her—not particularly pretty—feet. In between the main entrances there's a souvenir shop called "Platzhengst," where there are mostly Hippodrom items. In short: the Hippodrom is perhaps a bit more expensive and a bit more capricious than the other tents, but in exchange you'll have a wonderful time and meet stars of the Munich and international nightlife. Whatever the media may say about the Hippodrom host Sepp Krätz, he can certainly throw a party.

Music

Various bands with excellent repertoires make sure that there's a great mood in the tent. The main act is the "Münchner Zwietracht." They mainly play folk music, and can definitely make music for the people. They also play many classics, making for a special mood in the Hippodrom. Whether it's "Hey Jude," "Jump," or the Oktoberfest classic "Fürstenfeld," you'll be happy to jump into this world, and the music will ring in your ears long after.

Food and Drink

There's Spaten beer, the servers are quick and sometimes hectic because they want to give every table equal service and have a reputation to uphold. And they succeed. The food is excellent and the kitchen staff works on full power. In short:

143

The Hippodrom offers a special but still very satisfying Oktoberfest experience. A highlight: the Oktoberfest grilled chicken with good Bavarian spices by Alfons Schuhbck, spread with fresh alpine butter. As I said at the beginning, there is also the great champagne bar for a little something to tide you over. There is also champagne and spirits at the "Happy Hippodrom Bar" in the gallery. Next to it is the smokers' balcony.

Beer Garden

There's enough room for about 1,000 visitors in the beer garden of the Hippodrom. The warm orange and scarlet colors of the tent help you forget your regular life and the servers in the beer garden are quick and charming. Some old Munich natives like to reminisce about the horses, how they used to smoke cigars inside the tent, and in those days the mostly Australian audience would get into great brawls on the sandy floor. The Hippodrom garden is a great place to indulge in reminiscence, and you can take my word for it.

Seats: 4,300
Mood: Celebrity sightings and wild partying
Family Friendly: Absolutely not
Flirtation Factor: With good manners and good threads, very high
Beer: Spaten
Host: Sepp Krätz
Reservations: www.hippodrom-oktoberfest.de

Fischer-Vroni
Friendliness, Clothespins, and Fish on a Stick

The delicious smell of rainbow trout, mackerel, and char waft through the tent. From inside you can hear the pleasant hum. Not surprising, since for many Oktoberfest visitors there's nothing but Fischer-Vroni. A straightforward tent with a great atmosphere, that relaxed Bavarian charm, good Augustiner beer on tap, and a high flirtation factor. The front part of the roof is decorated with beautiful tiles. You'll notice the tent quickly, since it's the only one where a stork has made a nest year after year. It looks out over the festivities majestically and watches over the celebrating people. Right behind the main entrance on the left side, you can immerse yourself in a different world—the world of Fischer-Vroni.

Important Information

In 1904, the Munich gastronome Josef Pravida opened a small fish restaurant which quickly became popular. In 1907 a small fishing boat was put there. It's still there and it's a popular meeting spot. In the first year of the Federal Republic of Germany (Bundesrepublik Deutschland), 1949, the tent got a new owner, Karl Winter, and the name Fischer-Vroni. It isn't known whether there was ever an actual Veronika Fischer, but Philippine Winter, the widow of Karl Winter, was famous. Until her death in 1998 she was in the tent every day. In the same year, a

145

rearrangement of the seats was required by the fire code, and it was used as an opportunity to expand the tent by 700 seats.

Inner Life

Fischer-Vroni is one of the smaller tents at Oktoberfest, but it is particularly nice, homey, and cozy. It's no less nice on the inside: the mood, one could say, begins under the balconies while the tent is regenerating at night, before the charcoal fire is lit again and the elated ladies and gentlemen snatch up the 3,000 available seats. Here, truly no eye remains dry, whether from enthusiasm, sentimentality, or intoxication. And if you know your stuff, you know that here inside there are coveted clothespins for the lovely guests with the nickname or real name of the server written on them. And for a small fee, you can have something written on them to give to your dear friends. Our young friend Benedikt, who has been a core part of

our Oktoberfest group since 2011, received a clothespin from us with the inscription "wet behind the ears." He was very happy and showed how much he was moved by toasting us all with a fresh round.

Fans of nicotine can go outside on the east side of the tent to the smoking zone, which is covered in the event of rain. They've thought of everything at Oktoberfest.

On the second Monday of Oktoberfest, formerly called "mason Monday," same-sex groups meet in Fischer-Vroni for a "Prosecco Fest."

Music

The "Münchner Musikanten," under the leadership of Sepp Folger, make every visit to this tent a splendid occasion. I've never seen so many people spontaneously overcome with emotion, moved and elated by beer and music, as I have in Fischer-Vroni.

Mason Monday

On the second Monday of Oktoberfest, masons would invite their workers and colleagues to Oktoberfest. The masons were quite thirsty so sometimes there would be a misunderstanding and it would come to blows. This tradition has died out, both the fighting and the invitations from the masons.

Food and Drink

Logically, the best food on the menu at Fischer-Vroni is the fish on a stick. It's well-marinated fish grilled on a wooden stick. It's buttered so it turns out nice and crispy. It's traditionally served in paper. In my grandparents' time, it was wrapped in newspaper, so that you got something to read with your food, but you'd also eat a little ink. That's not done anymore, especially not in Fischer-Vroni. There is a street stand, though, where you can buy some good fish to take home with you after an Oktoberfest visit.

On the right side of the tent, the fish are prepared over an open fire in a 50-foot-long row. My personal recommendation is the whitefish, freshly caught in Lake Starnberg. Of course, you can choose almost any Oktoberfest delicacy from the Fischer-Vroni kitchen, from deer goulash to duck, to roast pork. Whatever your heart desires. And the Augustiner Edelstoff tastes good with all of it. On the last evening of Oktoberfest there's a clothing swap: the men serve in dirndls and the women in lederhosen.

Beer Garden

There is room for about 700 people in the small beer garden. But here, more than anywhere else, you'll be offered a seat, see friendly Bavarian faces both young and old, talk to lovely people from all different countries, joke with the cheerful servers, enjoy a fine Augustiner, share fish on a stick with a nice person, and just relax. When

---

Prosecco Fest in Fischer-Vroni

It's not as wild as the Bräurosl on Gay Sunday, but it still gets pretty gay in Fischer-Vroni on the second Monday. Countless people from the GLBT (gay, lesbian, bisexual, transgender) community all over the world meet here to celebrate. You should get there early, since it fills up quickly. More at www.rosawiesn.de

---

the sun is shining and the day begins to take shape in the beer garden of the Fischer-Vroni tent, you know just how beautiful life is.

Seats: 3,700
Mood: The best Munich craziness
Family Friendly: Very early in the day
Flirtation Factor: Super
Beer: Augustiner
Host: Hans and Silvia Stadtmüller
Reservations: www.fischer-vroni.de

Hofbräu-Festzelt
World Fame with International Flair

Oktoberfest is beloved by people around the world. A huge number of these visitors like to go to the Hofbräu tent, where there's a ton of things going on. In the middle of the tent is Aloisius with his harp. He's decorated with hops bines from Holledau which are attached to the roof of the Hofbräu tent. In no other tent will you meet such a variety of nationalities as here. Australians, Asians, Italians, French, Poles, Czechs, Kenyans, Puerto Ricans, Swiss, and also Germans raise their glasses here. And they do it often.

Important Information

The complement to the Munich Hofbräuhaus is the Hofbräu tent at Oktoberfest. Tourists of the world love the brick and mortar parent house in the city as well as the tent. But not only tourists. There are just as many natives. One of the symbols of this tent is the oversized Aloisius from the great short satire "A Municher in Heaven" by Ludwig Thoma. Before the Municher got to heaven, he was called Alois Hingerl, and since Thoma never wrote a part two, he's still sitting in the Hofbräuhaus, waiting for divine inspiration.

Most English-speaking visitors don't know the story of the Municher in Heaven. They only know that an oversized little man with a mustache, angel wings, a harp, and a red official's cap is floating on a cloud above their heads. For some reason, this figure reminds them of a mailman, so they often like to meet "under the postman." This always ends in frustration when visitors ask the Hofbräu servers where the postman is, and they have no clue what they're talking about. Alois Hingerl was a porter—number 172 at the Munich train station. Many women toss their undergarments to Aloisius, which is supposed to bring them good luck. Some come to Oktoberfest without any bra so they can flash their bare breasts to the music. They call this "tit-action." You'll only see this phenomenon in the Hofbräu tent, and the tent host

A Municher in Heaven

The 1911 story "A Municher in Heaven" by Ludwig Thoma is about the Munich porter Alois Hingerl, who makes a contract with such haste that he has a stroke and goes to heaven. He gets fed up quickly because there's no beer, only manna, and he has to spend all day exulting the glory of God. He gets grumpy and starts to complain. St. Petrus brings him to God. He complains again, and God sees no other option than to give him an envelope with godly counsel to bring to the  Bavarian government. Alois, who has become Aloisius in the meantime, is overjoyed and flies back home. As soon as he feels the Munich ground under his feet, he feels as if he's in heaven. Following his old habits, he heads to the Hofbräuhaus. He heads for his usual spot, finds it empty, and the waitress, Kathi, comes over to him . . . Happily, Aloisius orders a beer, and another beer, and another and forgets his letter and his assignment and orders another and another and another . . . And so, the Bavarian government is waiting to this day for some heavenly inspiration.

doesn't like it much, since it's called the Hofbräu tent, not the nudist tent. If you see pictures of naked people at Oktoberfest, you will rarely see the logos of any other breweries on the steins in the background. But the mood in the Hofbräu tent is always great. People eat, sing, dance, make out, and drink. What more could you want?

Inner Life

If you wanted to compare the mood of the Hofbräu tent with a musical experience, it would be a rock concert. A classical performance probably doesn't come to mind. It is the only tent with standing room in front of the music

stage, and there's room for 1,000. Hands with beer steins are always in the air, and one toast follows the next. It's boisterous, vivacious, and fun, and lots of people speak English. The local broadcaster "TV München" reports live daily from the Hofbräu tent so that everyone in Munich can enjoy the Hofbräu atmosphere even if they can't make it to Oktoberfest that day. Once, we met a group of five American tourists who wanted to order a typical Bavarian meal and asked us for advice. For fun, we said our favorite dish was "Betrunkenensalat"—drunken salad. All five ordered the fantasy dish that we had invented, with strong American accents of course. The server accepted the order like normal and returned shortly—with five more beer steins.

Music

The music of the "Plattlinger Isarspatzen" fits well in the highly intoxicating atmosphere. As soon as you walk into the tent, you feel the ecstasy, the urge to celebrate, you can literally smell it. It's a bit like descending into a dream that has existed since the beginning of time and that you dream again and again. Here it becomes real. And in short moments of clarity, you wake up from the dream, see the people around you and hear the music, briefly regain your sense, then wave the server over and order another Hofbräu.

Food and Drink

They serve very special delicacies here: skewered duck that melts in your mouth, roast venison, spare ribs, fresh garden salads, or the legendary cheese platter with the lovely name, "Steinbergs Kas-Variation." You can have a really good feast. My tip: the still-pink tenderloin with pepper béarnaise, roasted potatoes and homemade herbed cheese. And a good Hofbräu stein to go with it. It's like poetry.

But despite its name, in 1981 the Hofbräu tent actually served Paulaner for a few hours. The Hofbräu beer had run out, so the host asked his good friend Richard Süß-meier from the Armbrustschützen tent, and he was glad to help out with one of his 200-liter barrels.

Beer Garden

In the beer garden there are many more natives and locals from the surrounding countryside. For example, if I'm looking for my friend from Würmtal, I will probably find him in the outside area of the Hofbräu tent. There's room here for 3,000 people. The servers are like those at the "real" Hofbräuhaus: they merge classic Munich grumpiness with biting wit. And you can hear the bustling noise coming from inside.

Seats: 10,000

Mood: International jamboree

Family Friendly: On Tuesdays, 600 seats are held open for children and their parents from 11:00 to 3:00. There are also affordable food and drinks for families on the back balcony, with a good view of the tent.

Flirtation Factor: Clearly

Beer: Hofbräu

Host: Steinberg Family

Reservations: www.hb-festzelt.de

Käfer's Wies'n-Schänke
Exclusive Idyll

It looks like a mountain cabin. There are little niches and separate rooms all over, beautiful little decorations and all kinds of adornments. A truly lovingly-designed tent with a particular atmosphere. It's not for just any reason that the Käfer Wies'n-Schänke (Käfer or Käfer tent for short) has been a favorite meeting spot for celebrities for years. Along with the Hippodrom and the Weinzelt, it's one of the three so-called VIP tents. Because of the many nooks and crannies where you can hide and the cozy seating areas, the beer tent feeling is not as strong as in other tents. It's a great place to socialize, and you can spend some amazing evenings there.

Important Information

When all the other tents have to close, people are still partying here. The Käfer Wies'n-Schänke doesn't have to close its doors until 1:00 a.m. The lines of young, beautiful, and rich people waiting to get in the small side door to the late night Oktoberfest paradise are as long as you would think, and not just on the weekends. The door of nightclub has nothing on the door to the Käfer tent late in the evening during a warm Oktoberfest week. The Käfer is simply the place to be at Oktoberfest, if you're concerned with seeing and being seen. There's a correspondingly high number of journalists. Here you're always looking for who's there. Munich celebrities celebrate their

birthdays during Oktoberfest in the cozy, beautiful idyll in the country house whose sitting areas, winding rooms, and lovely decorations invite you to linger. The beer garden area is also lovely and, of course, blocked off. Once, a friendly man, probably in his early 60s and pretty drunk, tumbled from the interior into the beer garden of the Käfer tent. The door shut behind him and he couldn't get back in. He sat with a group of people and asked them in his Austrian dialect, "How do I get back in?" "You won't get back in!" laughed one of his neighbors, "But you can stay and sit with us. We have almost a whole dinner

platter left." The Austrian visitor was so happy that he bought a round for the whole table.

Inner Life

The Käfer came to Oktoberfest for the first time in 1971, as a teeny tiny spot with just 40 seats. Soon it got bigger and bigger, until finally the tent was built with wood like a mountain cottage. Inside, it's cozy and warm. It smells like wood and good food, there are idyllic sitting areas on the ground floor and upstairs, and there are ornaments and plants on the walls. The light is dim and encourages romantic conversation, sociable togetherness, amorous escapades, and hearty meals. The smoking area is on the bridge on the upper floor.

One time we were sitting on the first floor and the mood was like a hidden mountain cottage in the Alps. At the text table was a group of Spaniards who asked if we could take a picture of them. Of course we could, and then my friend noticed that three of the people in the group were members of the Spanish soccer team Real Madrid. We got into a conversation and before long some of us were sitting over there and some of the Spaniards were sitting by us. We joked and drank and there was hardly a dry eye by the end of the night.

Music

Perhaps the best and funniest cover band in the world is "Gary und Gerry" who play in the Käfer tent. A few years ago, they also played in the beer garden, but now they're totally in charge of the inside and make the tent into a happy mixture of ski lodge and saloon. Other bands play, of course, who also spread good cheer, but no one can top "Gary und Gerry."

Food and Drink

Feinkost Käfer is, after Dallmayr, the most important delicatessen in Munich, with its own associate catering business. Its main location is in Parsdorf, and since 2011 it can also be found in the Schrannenhalle market. Obviously, there is excellent food in the Käfer tent. It's not world famous for nothing. The dinner platter is lovingly and richly garnished, the duck is a dream, and

---

Seats: 3,000
Mood: Mountain cottage
Family Friendly: Not really
Flirtation Factor: Very high with good threads and a sassy mouth
Beer: Paulaner
Host: Michael and Clarissa Käfer
Reservations: www.feinkost-kaefer.de/oktoberfest

---

the various specialties from the cast iron pan will delight hungry stomachs. My tip: you have to try the saddle of venison. It'll drive you crazy.

Beer Garden

The beer garden is also decorated in a rustic style and you can reserve a table, which is not usual at the Oktoberfest beer gardens. Lots of wood, flowers, and embellishments create an Alpine atmosphere, the Paulaner is good, and the servers are lively and cheeky like country bartenders. The tent is very beloved and stays open later than the others, until 1 a.m., so you should get there very early or make a reservation, otherwise the beer garden will be packed and you won't get in.

Löwenbräu-Festzelt
Good Old Tradition

The Löwenbräu tent is welcoming, traditional, and Bavarian. The beer drinking lion by the entrance that roars "Löööööwenbräu" every few minutes inspires a natural thirst in every guest that must be quenched right away. Inside or out, you can't go wrong with the Löwenbräu tent. The friendly host is named Wiggerl Hagn and now and then you'll see him go by, waving. Then he smirks into his white Bavarian beard because he knows that what he's doing is good.

Important Information

The Löwenbräu tent is the home of the Munich Lion, since traditionally players and fans of the soccer team TSV 1860 Munich meet here, and their mascot is the lion. FC Bayern can be found over in the Käfer tent.

In the Löwenbräu tent, things are generally quite traditional. Here you'll see happy faces, rosy cheeks, and beautiful Trachten, and if you're familiar with the culture scene in Munich, you'll recognize the faces of cabaret performers, folk singers, and comedians. They know to cherish this treasure. Italian guests also like beer and the tent with the Löwenbräu brand. And, as I said, it's the home tent of the soccer team, and many of the workers are devoted lions. Even Wolfi, the man who serves

lemonade, is a lions fan. He laughs easily. The servers in this tent are particularly cheerful and personable, which doesn't keep them from being quick, hard workers. This is a tent for traditionalists and fans of sophisticated gossip—and sophisticated intoxication.

Inner Life

When you pass the tower where the thirsty lion can be seen from a distance, and walk under the other lion who drinks and repeats his catch phrase endlessly, you'll enter the tent that has been under the leadership of Wiggerl Hagn and his daughter Stephanie Spendler since 1979. It is a relatively large tent, but simply structured and pleasantly Bavarian. The arches are hung with yellow fabric and the boxes are in white and blue. Just like TSV 1860.

Music

Bert Hansmaier's band "Die Heldensteiner" knows what their audience wants. Traditional Wiesn Hits and international songs add a pleasant spice to the already excellent atmosphere.

Food and Drink

Coincidentally, this tent serves beer from the Löwenbräu brewery. The beer is just the right temperature, and there are delicious things to go with it, like grilled pork wurst with sauerkraut or the hearty leberwurst grill. And you absolutely can't forget the fried dough ("Kaiserschmarrn") served in a giant cast iron pan. Aaaaah!

Beer Garden

In the Löwenbräu tent beer garden there is a relaxed and welcoming atmosphere. It's the southernmost tent on Wirtsbudenstraße and it has the most southern temperament: people just let things come as they may. The servers are quick but relaxed, the beers are perfectly pulled, and the conversation is funny and substantial. And you can always talk about soccer.

Seats: 8,515
Mood: Tasteful and welcoming
Family Friendly: Absolutely
Flirtation Factor: Medium
Beer: Löwenbräu
Host: Ludwig Hagn and Stephanie Spendler
Reservations: www.loewenbraeuzelt.de

Ochsenbraterei
Elegant, Fine, with Spit-Roasted Beef

Every year during Oktoberfest, more than 100 oxen are consumed here. And to honor them after death and let the visitors know who the oxen were, a large sign informs you of the animals' names and how much they weighed. Like in the olden days, they are cooked on a spit and are tender and juicy when served.

Important Information

The focus here is the beef, and the initiated like to talk about the tent founder, Rössler Hansä, who invented a steaming, smoking, loud rotating machine to roast oxen. It was made of a steam engine mounted on four iron wheel and a rotating spit with a housing and vent. The modern spit is very quiet and doesn't spew out clouds of smoke, but just like back then, the beef tastes fabulous and is of the highest quality. The first ox roasted each year is Max (the name of the butcher) and the last is Richard (the name of the head chef). There's one ox that is around all week but isn't eaten: the plush ox August, who is very comfortable in the private box of the Haberl family.

Inner Life

The inner life of the Ochsenbraterei is very traditional,
which doesn't diminish the mood in the least. You can
eat in the boxes, dance in the middle, enjoy the nice view
from the gallery, whatever suits you. And history has been
written here. One time, the star chef Paul Bocuse visited
and enjoyed fine food and cool beer. At the 1972 Olympic games, the press and special guests were served here.
And because that went so well, the Ochsenbraterei was
in charge again four years later when the Olympiad was
in Innsbruck. The tent has a very Munich atmosphere,
and the audience is quite traditional and distinguished.
It's very colorful, it's cheerful even up in the gallery, and
you can have a ton of fun along with your roasted beef!

Music

The "Siegertsbrunner Blasmusik" play all day, and "Die Pucher" with Karl Flauger take the stage in the evening. Along with your culinary pleasures, you can sway and dance as well as smile and gallivant. Hermann Haberl, who was the tent host from 1980 to his death in February 2011, always played the Bavarian anthem on his trumpet on the last evening of Oktoberfest. Finally, a moon lantern was carried through the whole darkened tent up to the band. A beautiful, melancholy, and dreamy finale. Since his death, the six trumpeters of the band carry on this beloved tradition.

Food and Drink

While an ox is growing, intermuscular fat develops in the meat which has a positive effect on the later taste of the meat, keeping it juicy and and tender when roasted. There's the classic, marbled beef with homemade red wine sauce and potato salad, the same with the slightly more expensive loin or a filet with garden vegetables and scalloped potatoes. Good Spaten beer is served with it and rounds off the delicious taste. All the oxen come from nearby Gut Karlshof, where the best quality is guaranteed.

Beer Garden

Let the day fade away in one of the 1,500 seats, drink a Spaten, and leave your daily life behind. You can do all that in the lovely beer garden of the Ochsenbraterei. You'll be served well and quickly but without rush, the visitors are mostly from Munich and surrounding areas, and it's easy to have a chat. And if you sit in the front near the entrance, you'll be treated to a great mechanical show: two southern Bavarians with traditional hats turn the spits over the fire tirelessly from morning to night. That'll work up your appetite!

Seats: 7,500
Mood: Tasteful fun
Family Friendly: Yes
Flirtation Factor: Relatively high in the center area
Beer: Spaten
Host: Anneleise Haberl and Antje Schneider
Reservations: www.ochsenbraterei.de

Festhalle Schottenhamel
Fun and Pure Tradition

First of all, let's be clear: the name Schottenhamel has nothing to do with men in skirts with bagpipes. It is the oldest tent at Oktoberfest. In the Schottenhamel is where the Munich mayor officially taps the first keg. Other points in history have been written here, too: years before he was a famous scientist, a young Albert Einstein installed the electricity. Here, you can flirt for all you're worth. You're also guaranteed to see beautiful dirndls. This tent is very beloved by the younger set. The Schottenhamel has been around since 1867, and the two cousins, Christian and Michael, handle the responsibility of their surname with bravura.

Important Information

What is today the Schottenhamel tent was originally just a small wooden shack behind the King's tent. That was in 1867. Each year the tent founder, Michael Schottenhamel, thought up a new expansion. The band of a military orchestra played, and when they took a break, selected artists took the stage so that continuous amusement was provided. The tent quickly became a favorite meeting spot for students, those interested in culture, artists, aristocrats, citizens of all classes, and is still a magnet for young, good-looking people ready to celebrate. Wimmer Dammerl, erstwhile Munich mayor, introduced

the ritual of the official tapping here in 1950. Since then, Oktoberfest begins just like this book: with "Ozapft is!"

Inner Life

It's hard to believe that just 150 years ago, the Schottenhamel tent was a little shack with only 50 seats. Today it's more like 10,000. The inner life of the tent is like the dramaturgy in a good play, a song, or a good movie. The morning in Schottenhamel is relaxed. It starts to fill up in the afternoon, and the atmosphere climbs gradually. More and more young people appear, dressed to kill, and it eventually becomes enthusiastic, euphoric, and energetic. This situation lasts for hours until the climax, and for the finale everyone clinks glasses again, newly in-love couples head home, and there are declarations of brotherhood and friendship. After the last song, the crowd disperses into the night to enjoy the Munich nightlife or to rest for the next Schottenhamel visit. Smoking is allowed on the outer balcony and over the main entrance. Once a tipsy young man with a foreign dialect couldn't find his seat and he asked a friendly man in lederhosen if he could help. The man was very accommodating and he knew the tent well. Before long, he led the young man back to his friends. But the young man didn't know that the friendly man was no less than the tent host himself—Christian Schottenhamel!

Music
The "Orchester Otto Schwarzfischer," despite the name, aren't concerned with fish in unknown waters, but rather with spreading good cheer with energetic music. Under the leadership of Christian Sachs, the musicians provide excellent background music for the friskiness of the young Schottenhamel audience.

Food and Drink
There's Spaten on tap and to go with it there's Bavarian beef loin in a green pepper sauce with roasted potatoes from the grill or a crispy half duck with spicy red

cabbage and fresh potato dumplings, for example. The romaine salad with corn-fed chicken breast, parmesan-garlic dressing, and cherry tomatoes with fresh wood stove bread is also sensational.

Beer Garden

Young and old mix outside. You also see visitors from other countries and the servers are good and speedy. Since the Schottenhamel has long been attractive to young men, the mood in the beer garden is also a bit younger and louder, which the older visitors know is part of the charm. Fresh cheer goes well with a fresh beer.

Seats: 10,000
Mood: Party
Family Friendly: In the beer garden
Flirtation Factor: Terrific
Beer: Spaten
Host: Christian and Michael F. Schottenhamel
Reservations: www.festzelt.schottenhamel.de

Schützen-Festzelt
Bulls-eye with Atmosphere and Tradition

It's hidden right at the foot of the Bavaria statue, and in a drunken state it can be hard to find the entrance on the first try. You need an insider's tip not just for the location, but for the tent itself. It's a traditional meeting place for sport shooters, the upper classes, and nobility. But it's also been a big party tent for quite a few years. Here you'll find old-fashioned mixed with modern. The big balcony is always covered with geraniums. That sort of floral decoration is only known in the Alpine foothills. And every year the Oktober marksmanship competition is held here.

Important Information

This tent was originally a true shooting range where various shooting competitions were held. The precursor to this tent was founded in 1926 with seats for 400, but the culinary offering at the time was pretty second-tier. The main tent was rather simple and drafty. Most of the shooters only came over to shoot and drank in neighboring tents where there was decent food. In the beginning of the 1960s, the tent was refreshed and within 40 years it grew into a really, nice festival tent that was inaugurated in 2004. Now it has a modern shooting range and the culinary delights are outstanding! In addition

to the sport shooters and their bands, simple citizens, and traditionalists, a secret society called the "Guglmen" meet here. They have made it their assignment to protect the memory of King Ludwig II of Bavaria.

Inner Life

A few years ago, this tent was the meeting place for the noble, the ancient, and old soldiers, but today young people also find their way to this tent. It has a beautiful ceiling and an exceptional, warm atmosphere. If you come inside, you'll stay, since there's something magical about it. Is it the mixture of good Löwenbräu beer with its malty scent and the colorful assortment of guests of all classes and regions? Is it the low number of seats in the relatively

> "A licentious, immoral nest of fanaticism, rudeness, and stubbornness, full of icons, dumplings, and radish-sellers..."
> *Gottfried Keller on Munich*

large room (specifically 4,300)? Who knows? What I do know that all my visits have been very memorable and I can only recommend that you pay this tent a visit.

Music

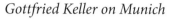

The "Niederalmer" play here, and play almost exclusively rock and pop. The concept works: the crowd is lively and tipsy, the party is wild, and it's always fun to see ancient old men celebrating along with students, counts, earls, barons, and nobility!

Food and Drink

The crispy half duck from Baron von Lüttitz from Mangfalltal with red cabbage and apples and roast potatoes is worth a visit to the Schützen-Festzelt all by itself. An excellent, famous delicacy is the suckling pig, partly marinated in malt beer and partly as a roll roast with caraway sauce. You also can't miss the beef roulade with ham, onions, and vinegar pickles served with mashed potatoes! Of course there are also vegetarian options. A freshly tapped Löwenbräu to go with it, and the party can start!

Beer Garden

A bit over 1,000 seats and a view of the Bavaria statue attract fans of the Schützen tent each year. You sit comfortably, enjoy respectable service, and very often meet old native Bavarians who love to reminisce about the past. You're on the edge of Oktoberfest and yet right in the heart of it. You can gaze far into the distance and leave the burdens and stress of your daily life behind you.

Seats: 5,500
Mood: Aristocratic Oktoberfest jamboree with atmosphere and real shooting
Family Friendly: Yes
Flirtation Factor: High in the evenings
Beer: Löwenbräu
Host: Eduard Reinbold and sons (who also own the "Hotel Drei Löwen" and "Zum Franziskaner" in Munich)
Reservations: www.schuetzen-festzelt.de

Kuffler's Weinzelt
Choice Wines and Fine Food

The wine tent is a wine tent and not a beer tent and so it a different sort of beast. It is certain, however, that it's a place to celebrate, that it stays open until 1:00 a.m., and that it serves wine. They also serve weiss beer, but it is pricey. If you're going to the wine tent, you should drink wine. It's a good place to do it, since they offer a very good variety of wines—and there are plenty of very good-looking people. If you put in the effort, you could probably make a good match over a bottle of wine. And if you're a star watcher: there are some hidden here, too.

Important Information

The tent used to be called the "Nymphenburg Sparkling Wine Tent." They had drinks aside from sparkling wine, of course, select wines and Bavarian food. In 1999 the Kuffler family inherited the tent from the wine cellar. The name "wine tent" was quickly established among the people, so they made it official. The rustic furnishings go well with the large selection of truly excellent international wines.

Inner Life

The inside of the tent is furnished with a lot of wood and cozy corners. By the way, the wood is over a hundred years old and exudes that pleasant smell of wine barrels and wine cellars. The boxes are very cozy, the mood is excellent, and the flirtation factor is very high. Dim lanterns are hung from big, round fixtures and add to the pleasant atmosphere. This tent is like a country house with visitors who love a good drink. The mood is fabulous, everyone is dancing and laughing, feasting and singing. An Oktoberfest tent that's a little different—and merry from wine, not beer.

Music

A total of three bands play from 11 a.m. to midnight and get the merry crowd pumped up. The "Sumpfkröten" play until 4:30 p.m., the delightfully Bavarian "Blechblosn" play from 5:00 to 8:30, and the "Högl Fun Band" play from 9:00 to midnight.

Food and Drink

They offer high quality bottled wine in addition to many wines by the glass. All of the wines by the glass are also available as a half-liter spritzer. Beside Arneis Blangé from Piemont and an phenomenal Riesling, there is a  decent range of white wines and a small but fine selection of red wines from France, Austria, Germany, and Italy. You can also encourage high spirits with sparkling wine, prosecco, and champagne. Wonderful cheeses are also offered to go with the wine, plus a respectable dinner and good salad. My recommendations from the cold menu: the Mediterranean vegetable plate with grilled baby artichoke, zucchini, pepper, and fennel in olive oil and herbs, served warm with a crispy baguette. There are hearty dishes from Kuffler's house butcher, simple cooking from Spatenhaus an der Oper, delicacies from Haxnbauer, a fine selection from Seehaus, and top-quality dishes from the menu of Mangostin. Examples? Truffle  tortellini with freshly grated summer truffles, six giant Pacific oysters on ice with pumpernickel bread, or "Papa Joe's Selection" of prawns, chicken wings, spring rolls, tempura bites, and satay kebabs served with Japanese coleslaw, peanut dip, sweet and sour chili sauce, and Thai plum sauce. They also have excellent roast potatoes. And we can't forget the dessert menu, from the warm plum pastries with sugar glaze and whipped cream, to the cheese crepes with apricot preserves. The crowning finish is the spirits from the Schleierseer liquor manufacturer Latenhammer, served in sweet little flip-top bottles. My recommendation: the apricot brandy. That will brighten your day!

Beer Garden

The outside area of the wine tent invites you to relax and linger. There is room for about 500 people who want to relax outside in the fresh air for a while longer before going into the actual tent. In 2006 the garden was newly designed and is now a beautiful Frankish wine garden with high pergolas, garden benches, and a round, open garden pavilion designed by architect Gerhard Zobler. In such a pretty, cozy atmosphere, the wine tastes twice as good.

Seats: 3,000
Mood: Gourmet explosion and country house party
Family Friendly: No
Flirtation Factor: Sensational
Beer: Paulaner weiss beer until 9:00 p.m.
Host: Roland, Doris, and Stephan Kuffler
Reservations: www.weinzelt.com

Winzerer Fähndl
Stars and Coziness

You can see it from almost everywhere at Oktoberfest: the rotating Paulaner beer stein. It happens to be 20 feet tall and attracts droves of people. The name of this beautiful tent originally comes from the crossbow shooting guild of the same name from Tölz, which in turn was named after the he hero of the Bavarian peasant's revolt and knight, Kaspar Winzerer. The guild formerly had their main Oktoberfest meeting spot here. The crossbow shooters moved to the Armbrustschützen tent years ago, but the name remains for the Paulaner tent.

Important Information

The Winzerer Fähndl is located more or less at the feet of the Bavaria statue; the two gaze reverently upon each other. The tent was always worth a visit, but it has admittedly become more charming since its renovation in 2010. The big window in the front facade is beautiful and gives you a gorgeous view of the beer garden. The free-standing interior has a lavish span and allows for a fabulous view of the band from all sides.

Inner Life

It's very cozy and upbeat in here. The host, Peter and Arabella Pongratz, have done their best to make the inside of their tent lovely and unforgettable for visitors. Every visit is an experience. The tent is, as stated above, is very roomy due to its freestanding construction and resulting lack of support columns, the boxes are linked by little stairs, and there's a good mood all day. The Hamburg artist, Jean-Pierre Kunkel created the funny, cheeky Bavarian illustrations that decorate the "Nockherberg" box, the "Brauerei" box, the "Haus" box, and the "Brauerei" balcony. Eighty-five hundred people fit in the bright, airy tent. From time to time you see celebrities in this tent, for example the members of FC Bayern. It's a nice tent to walk around in, and there is a grandious solution for smokers: the balcony on the second floor not only allows tobacco, it also offers the most beautiful view at Oktoberfest—a direct view of the Bavaria statue.

Music

The music is pleasantly diverse and very atmospheric. There's good Bavarian concert music all day, and in the evening the cozy tent becomes a hopping party with the best mood music. The "Nockherberger" play with a rotating lineup. Since there are all ages in the audience, the music choices are very diverse. There's everything from classic rock to Schlager to good old Wiesn Hits.

Food and Drink

Delicious Paulaner Oktoberfest beer with a velvety foam is served here. The servers are very fast and the beer is very drinkable. To go with it, the kitchen director, Andreas Geitl (multiple gold medal winner at the "Bavarian Cuisine" competition) prepares culinary high-  lights like marinated boiled beef with potato-pumpkin vinaigrette, cherry tomatoes, and radishes or the excellent pretzel Guglhupf with vegetables in parmesan cream, well-seasoned roast chicken, plenty of cold dishes, and well-glazed veal shank. My favorite: the crispy suckling pig in beer sauce! Bon appetit!

Seats: 11,000
Mood: Good atmosphere for young and old
Family Friendly: Yes
Flirtation Factor: Decent
Beer: Paulaner
Host: Peter and Arabella Pongratz
Reservations: www.winzerer-faehndl.com

Beer Garden

Like inside, the outside area has probably the most colorful mix of people at Oktoberfest. Guests of all ages, origins, and both genders romp about and toast with wonderful Paulaner Oktoberfest beer. The atmosphere is cheerful and fun, it's easy to start up conversations, and the servers are charming. The beer garden is very big with 2,500 seats. The nicest spot is under the big balcony with a view of the Bavaria statue on the south side of the tent. My favorite spot at Oktoberfest!

Smaller Tents

Sometimes Oktoberfest is totally booked up in advance, but there is always somewhere to go. With a little bit of ingenuity, you can get a reservation shortly before or even during Oktoberfest week by switching to a small tent. They are more personal and homey. Many people find that the smaller tents offer a more old-fashioned but more authentic Oktoberfest feeling that creates the traditional charm of Oktoberfest. The small tents are very diverse and offer many alternatives: wild parties, traditional beer tents, rustic, homey, or contemplative. In the small tents, you can enjoy lovingly prepared Bavarian food in a peaceful atmosphere. And of course, there is refreshing Oktoberfest beer. Often, you'll be served by the tent hosts themselves.

Ammer Roast Chicken and Duck

This tent was founded in 1885 by the poultry seller from the Viktualien market, Joseph Ammer. That makes it possibly the oldest roast chicken stand in the world. Here, you can get high-quality chickens and ducks not

A hot little number.

only from a street booth, but also inside the tent. Can I tell you a secret? I believe that this is the best chicken at Oktoberfest. But don't tell anyone I told you. The Ammer tent has over 450 seats inside and 470 in the beer garden. "Die Hinterberger Musikanten" provide entertainment in the form of traditional Bavarian music, and in the evening there's party music with "Claudia Sommer & Band." Augustiner Edelstoff is on tap. The Ammer tent also has the best paintings at Oktoberfest on its food cart with scenes from the legendary German TV series "Monaco Franze" by Helmut Dietl. What does that have to do with the tent? Apparently, both involve the saying, "A little bit goes a long way!" Diana the bathroom attendant, whose apron says "WC Angel," agrees. Every evening at 8:30 she sings Schlager and Wiesn Hits for her cheering audience.

Reservations: www.ammer-wiesn.de

Heimer Roast Chicken and Duck

Nestled between Hacker and Schottenhamel is the Heimer Roast Chicken and Duck tent. This spot is great for a short visit, a company party, or a family outing. Their specialty is crispy duck on a stick, rubbed with a special (secret) spice mixture and grilled. There are also potato dumplings, celery salad, and red cabbage. There is purposely no music to make the tent a contrast to the wild party tents. Here you just hear the sounds of the guests and the bustling workers.

Reservations: www.heimer-entenbraterei.de

Heinz Wurst and Roast Chicken

To the left of Schottenhamel is Heinz. There are as many seats in this lovely little tent as days in the year. Families, coworkers, and solo visitors appreciate the cozy and familiar atmosphere, good Paulaner beer, select wines, prosecco, schnapps, non-alcoholic drinks, wonderful soups, fine wurst, perfect dinners, excellent fried and roasted foods, And a small but excellent selection of desserts. Their motto: "Go over to Heinz and get something fine!"

Reservations: www.heinz-huehnerbraterei.de

Poschner's Roast Chicken and Duck

Directly next to the Hacker beer garden is the Poschner Roast Chicken and Duck tent. Head in for a good snack or a lovely evening. What's special about it: there are hostesses who bring you right to your table. The tables are always set and the servers add to the very friendly atmosphere. They take care of all the creature comforts: whether you want a hearty chicken soup, a double poultry spread with salad and pomegranate dressing, or chicken, duck, and turkey cutlets with a huge selection of sides and good Hacker-Pschorr beer and brandy. My recommendation: the South Tirol William Christ Pear Brandy. It gives you the feeling of having a mouthful of fresh, ripe fruit.

Reservations: www.poschners.de

Wildmoser Roast Chicken and Duck

The Wildmoser Roast Chicken and Duck tent has between the Hofbräu tent and the Armbrustschützen tent since 1981. It is a lovely, small, relaxed tent with room for

320 people. "Die Zwei" play cheerful, entertaining music here and there is good food in the kitchen. They offer excellent standards like duck, chicken, or salad along with delicious soups. Their specialty: organic chicken breast filet in sesame bread-ing with pan-cooked vege-tables and rice timbale. (For your information: a timbale is a small, round, flat plate.) To drink, there is good Hacker-Pschorr beer, wine, prosecco, and a small selection of schnapps.

Reservations:

www.huehner-und-entenbraterei-wildmoser.de

Zum Stiftl

It used to be called the Wienerwald tent. Lorenz Josef Stiftl was already the manager, and then he took over with his wife, Maria. It is decorated like a rustic ski lodge. This small but fine tent has room for 360 peo-ple and a huge selection of appetizers, desserts, entrees, and kids' meals. I can highly recommend the Swiss tur-key wurst salad with cheese and onions. A unique dish is the fresh porcini mushrooms with pretzel dumplings in herb cream. And for dessert I can only recommend the weiss beer tiramisu with fresh fruit, served in a jar.

There's cool Hacker-Pschorr, white and red wine, prosecco, champagne, and schnapps to drink, and the house schnapps, "Rachengurgler." You can also pick up a delicious half chicken "on the way" from the street booth. Many spontaneous and random meetings have occurred here. Who knows how many married couples started out in the legendary spot?

Reservations: www.stiftl.de

Wirtshaus im Schichtl

The magic theater "Auf geht's beim Schichtl" has existed at Oktoberfest since the year 1869 and is one of the oldest Oktoberfest landmarks. Since 2001, Schichtl boss Manfred Schauer has operated a small beer tent with 120 seats next to his show booth. They have Spaten and Franziskaner weiss beer, plus all the meat comes from the organic farm Hermannsdorfer in Glonn near Munich, which means you get the highest quality from a known organic producer. The menu is complex; there is something for everyone. While heads are rolling in the theater next door and Ringo Praetorius is attending to his executioner's duties with the guillotine, the guests here are enjoying very friendly and personal service. This little tent is highly recommended, independent of the Schichtl show. The very funny "Zipfi Zapfi Buam" play daily.

Reservations: www.schichtl.by

Feisinger's Cheese and Wine

The cheese figure at the entrance is reminiscent of the old video game character, Pac-Man. But there are no video games here. There are just 100 seats in this small tent, and on warm days you can enjoy the specialties from one of the 90 seats in the beer garden while catching some sun.

You can get hearty cheese specialties here: from Swiss raclette, Allgäuer cheese noodles, and Swabian finger noodles with sauerkraut to fresh-baked  Alsatian flammekueche. They have everything to do with cheese, but also offer noodle and potato dishes. To go with these, there's good Frankish wine and Achenseer brandy. Only half the seats can be reserved, so it's always worth checking in.

Reservations: www.wiesnzelt.de

Burtscher's Bratwurst

Burtscher's Bratwurst tent is right in front of the Bräurosl and is the smallest tent at Oktoberfest. There's room for up to 90 guests. It's very cozy inside, and during the day it's rather quiet and reserved. On weekends, the mood goes up when the "Original Rochaholixs Buam" play every evening from Wednesday through Sunday. There are Bavarian treats like daily fresh weisswurt, along with Spaten and Franziskaner weiss beer.

Reservations: www.wiesn-bratwurst.de

Wildstuben

The Wildstuben is on Schaustellerstraße. The tent looks like a Bavarian forest cabin with hand-carved Tyrolean figures on the façade. There are 200 seats, a real chimney, deer antlers, and nice little corners to sit in. Chandeliers provide homey lighting. Up in the gallery you can watch the goings on in the tent and the brisk activity outside. On the roof a funny boar is roasting on a spit. There is wild boar to eat as wurst or on a roll. There are also plenty of other specialties along with Augustiner beer, good brandies, wines, and prosecco. There's also daily live music.

Reservations: www.wildstuben.de

Glöckle Wirt

As of recently, the Glöckle Wirt can be found to the left of the Winzerer Fähndl. Here there are fine Bavarian delicacies, many vegetarian dishes, and refreshing juice spritzers, but also delicious Spaten-Franziskaner beer. Every day after 7:00 p.m. the band "Schubiduo" plays. There are just 100 seats. The host is named Hanns-Werner Glöckle. On the walls there are nice old instruments, sleds, kitchen tools, jars, and oil paintings. A really lovely little tent.

Reservations: www.gloeckle-wirt.de

Zur Bratwurst

Directly beside the Toboggan there is a tent in the style of a Frankish Fachwerk house with a copper roof and decorative stars. It has two levels and space for 180 visitors. In the beer garden is room for 80 more. The famous roasted bratwurst taste especially good. They are grilled over an open beechwood fire which gives them a unique flavor. Visitors from the whole world love them. Of course there is also the totally normal bratwurst, otherwise the name would be nonsense. Andi Gaßner makes outstanding oxen sausage and there is weisswurst from the Schelkopf butcher. Zur Bratwurst

I have my humble means.

is the wildest of all the small tents. Here people let loose and dance on the tables. There's Augustiner to drink.

Reservations: www.zur-bratwurst.de

Haxenbraterei Hochreiter

This tent is located between the Hacker and HB tents. Dieter Hochreiter will never tell the secret spice mix he uses to season his pork and veal knuckles. The host keeps this closely guarded family secret in his head. The only thing that he'll say is that dark beer plays an important role in the sauce. The grilled pork and veal knuckles are served with cabbage and potato dumplings. There is Löwenbräu and Franziskaner weiss beer to drink. The Hochreiters also own the nostalgic Weiss Beer Carousel, the biggest portable carousel bar in the world. It turns very slowly, but it does turn. It takes over 11 minutes for a full rotation and there's room for 130 people on it.

Reservations: www.haxenbraterei.com

Kalbs-Kuchl

Since 2008 the Kalbs-Kuchl has been next to the Bräurosl. And you really can't miss it: A huge flag with meat and dumplings on it stimulates your appetite from afar. The tent is decorated like an Alpine cabin with a room of old Swiss pine and seats for 300 visitors. They offer delicious dishes centered on veal: roast veal from their big grill, boiled veal filet, Wiener schnitzel, and many others. All day there is folk music and in the evening there is mood music. There is Spaten and Franziskaner weiss beer on tap.

Reservations: www.kabls-kuchl.de

Münchner Knödelei

With their round shape, Bavarian dumplings are something cozy, yet sensual. And here there are many rolled each day. The Knödelei (dumpling house) is between the Olympia and the Ferris wheel and has seats for 90 guests outside and 180 inside. Here you can indulge in dumplings—meat dumplings, cheese dumplings, mushroom dumplings, beet dumplings, spinach dumplings, banana dumplings, plum dumplings . . . There's even a square pretzel dumpling. It's filled with sheep's cheese and is served on a "vegetable medley." Official description of the square dumpling: "Because of its squareness, the square dumpling is stable on your plate and has a low risk of dirtying the clothing of the dumpling eater or his immediate area." You can drink Paulaner with it and the band "Take Five" plays after 6:00 p.m.

Reservations: www.muenchner-knoedelei.de

Vinzenz Murr Metzgerstubn

The name Vinzenz Murr has a long tradition in Munich and can't be left out of Oktoberfest. Since 2010, the host Evi Brandl is back after a two-year hiatus with a completely redesigned Metzgerstubn, a recent name change. The Metzgerstubn is right of the Armbrustschützen tent in the front part of Wirtsbudenstraße. Beside golden Paulaner beer, they serve fine wurst specialties: old Bavarian meat dishes like sour veal lungs prepared according to the old family recipe are on the menu along with original Munich weisswurst, original Munich pork bratwurst, crispy roast pork from Hofgut Schwaige, tender sirloin steak, and homemade tartare. Many classic Munich foods that had been unjustly forgotten are on the daily menu here, and at the street booth you can find fresh Leberkäs, crispy roast pork, and pork belly that you can take into the beer garden. In the Vinzenz Murr Metzgerstubn you will find live music, homey decorations, and seats for 130 people. You can also see many historical exhibits about Munich butcher history of founders Rosa and Vinzenz Murr.

Reservations: www.vinzenzmurr.de

Coffee Tents

Many visitors want a piece of
cake with a cup of coffee, a glass
of prosecco, or a good cock-
tail after an Oktoberfest adventure. For them, there is a
variety of things on offer in the coffee tents. In the afternoon, it stays rather dignified, but the corks start pop-
ping in the evening. Unfortunately the nice Café Diestler
(perhaps more known to some as the "Café of the Beautiful Munich Girl") isn't around anymore. It was decorated with 36 portraits of comely Munich women from
the famous beauty collection of King Ludwig I of Bayern.
Today the Café Kaiserschmarrn from the Rischart company stands in its spot.

Bodo's Café

The ex-Narrhalla Fasching Prince Bodo E. Miller, cake
designer and doughnut specialist, opened his café tent in
1993 after having operated a coffee stand for five years.
The tent is between Augustiner and Ochsenbraterei, right
behind the Ammer if you come from Wirtsbudenstraße.
The tent with its motley decorations offers various

Ausgezogene

Ausgezogene are beloved Alpine doughnuts, also known as "Kiachl" ("little cakes"). The bakers used to stretch the dough over their knees, so people would say that whoever had the strongest knees would make the best Ausgezogene. The dough should be so thin in the middle, the old wisdom says, that a young bakery worker could read a love letter through the dough.
Ausgezogene are traditionally dusted with powdered sugar, sometimes filled with raisins, and sometimes have some cinnamon or vanilla added.

strudels, a rich selection of bakery items, and fabulous Ausgezogene in addition to coffee.

Aside from various kinds of doughnuts in Bodo's style, there are wonderful apple, cream, and cherry strudels served with homemade vanilla sauce. You can also get moist poppy strudel with cream, ice cream, and other sweet specialties. Their coffee is also very good, and you can enjoy a cappuccino in between two beers. In the evening, the "Las Vegas Show Band" plays and cocktails are mixed. Celebrities like to visit Bodo's Café Tent, too. Bodo knows everyone, whether soccer players or movie stars.

Reservations: www.bodos.de

Café Kaiserschmarrn

From the outside it looks a bit like a Disneyworld gingerbread house: a cookie castle in the land of cakes. The Munich pastry specialist, Rischart, has a good spot at Oktoberfest across from the Weinzelt. From outside you can see coffee cups with eyes and mouths, living spoons, and all kinds of sweet tidbits on the towers of the Kaiserschmarrn castle. Here you can feast to your heart's content. There are countless bakery specialties and delicious Kaiserschmarrn, a kind of fried pancake, in nine (!) variations. In the evening there is live music and cocktails. The Kaiserschmarrn tent has the only catwalk at Oktoberfest, in the form of a free-swinging bridge over the guests' heads. The catwalk is mostly used by the band, but you can also watch pretty young singers on it. The later it gets, the more energy the band puts in. It gets pretty wild on and under the catwalk. When the Aperol Spritz cocktails come out, people start dancing and kissing. A fun event: in remembrance of the wedding of Crown Prince Ludwig and Princess Therese von Saxony-Hildburghausen, they cut a wedding cake in Café Kaiserschmarrn every day at 2:00 p.m.

Cheerful crown from the Kaiserschmarrn Tent.

Reservations: www.rischart.de

Café Mohrenkopf

The lovely Café Mohrenkopf has existed at Oktoberfest since 1950 and it can be found right behind the Bräurosl. It's the only Oktoberfest tent with its own pastry kitchen, which means all the cakes and tortes are baked in the tent. The still-warm cakes and the homemade apple strudel attract gourmands from around the world. And of course, you should taste the "Mohrenkopf," a meringue covered in chocolate and filled with fresh whipped cream. The inside of the tent seats 400 guests and is decorated in the icing colors blue, ecru, and rose. On weekdays after 10:00 a.m. and weekends after 9:00 a.m. there are pretzels, baked good, and the best Dallmayr coffee. In the back of the tent there is a cocktail bar. In the evening the Munich party band "Flat Out" rocks the tent, and you can dance.

Reservations: www.cafe-mohrenkopf.eu

Schiebl's Kaffeehaferl

The tent is located right next to the Ammer tent and has room for about 100 people. There is intentionally no music so that you can take a moment to relax with a nice piece of cake. I can particularly recommend the exquisite apple cake. It's prepared traditionally and exudes coziness and familiar peacefulness.

Haferl

In the Bavarian-Austrian dialect, a big mug is called a "Haferl." It comes from the old word for a baker, "Hafner." The large earthenware bowls that could be found in every kitchen back then were called "Häfen." In Bavarian, it transformed into "Haferl." There are two theories on origin of the term Haferl shoe: some say it's playfully derived from the coffee "Haferl," and some say that the Alpine mountain shoes came into fashion with the English in the nineteenth century and were sold under the name "half shoes."

They serve fresh Irish coffee, doughnuts, apple strudel, and steamed buns. The Kaffeehaferl is a very peaceful place where you can take a break and relax with a cup of coffee, a glass of wine, or an Irish coffee.

Reservations: www.schiebls-cafebetreibe.de

Wiesn Guglhupf

The little tent in the form of a giant Guglhupf (Bundt cake) is on Schaustellerstraße, right behind the

Theresienwiese U-Bahn station. This tent rotates so that all the visitors can take in everything around them while peacefully enjoying a piece of Guglhupf with coffee, tea, or a good tall drink. And don't worry, it turns so slowly that you can get on and off without problems. The open construction invites you to sit practically outside in nice weather. If it's a bit cool out, the transparent sides are closed, but the 360° panoramic view remains.

There's room for about 60 people. Since a maximum of 60 percent of the tables can be reserved, it's always worth checking to see if there's a table free. The Guglhupf is a good place to go for a nightcap, since it closes at 11:30 p.m. The beer brandy served in a small bottle is very good.

The house specialty is raisin Guglhupf. It tastes home-made. And it is. There are also other Guglhupf creations with plums, beer, egg liqueur, and savory variations like tomato, salmon, or zucchini.

Reservations: www.wiesn-guglhupf.de

Traditional Amusement

Carnival Rides at Oktoberfest

It's easy to forget, but next to Wirtsbudenstraße with all the beer tents there is also Schaustellerstraße. Here you will find countless carnival rides, shooting booths, show booths, and entertainment. The offerings are many. You should decide in advance whether your stomach can handle the sometimes wild rides and mentally take inventory of what you've eaten and drunk. When that question is

Come into the menagerie!

Spinning

In many of the carnival rides you spin around and are tossed from left to right. It's fun, but here, too, you should consider your personal condition before you get on. Sometimes you'll go upside down, and you should take care for your own health and for others, that you don't empty your stomach along with your pockets. For some people, spinning around has positive side effects; they feel their spirit reawakened and it works like a fountain of youth on them. For women, this effect seems  to work in a special way, which you can tell by their exuberant whooping. Children apparently tolerate spinning around better than adults do.

cleared up, you can let your desires take charge, let go, and enjoy the ride.

As a child, I did everything my parents would let me, and as a youth, everything I could afford with my pocket money. Later, I discovered the joys of the beer tent and now I only use Schaustellerstraße when a nice young lady asks politely. But then it's straight back to the beer tent.

The show booths and carousels are always changing, and you should take a look for yourself, see what speaks to you, and decide spontaneously what you'd like to do. Tuesday is Family Day, and there are reduced prices on rides, booths, and food stands until 6:00 p.m. At show booths and rides with signs indicating so, there are reduced prices on weekdays between 10:00 a.m. and 3:00 p.m. There are also lunch specials in almost all the tents at that time. I'm going to introduce a small selection of rides, booths, and entertainment. I've divided them into two categories: common things that are particularly fun at Oktoberfest, and things that can only be found at Oktoberfest. I make no claim that this is an exhaustive list.

Common Things That Are Particularly Fun at Oktoberfest

An Oktoberfest visit without a Ferris wheel ride is like a beer without head. The big Ferris wheel at the southern end of Wirtsbudenstraße is a Munich landmark and one of the long-lasting Oktoberfest attractions. In the

seventeenth and eighteenth centuries, there were similar precursors in Asia and Russia which were called "Russian Wheels."

The modern Ferris wheel is made of steel and was developed in 1960. The Munich Ferris wheel belonging

Great events cast a long shadow …

to the Willenborg family was constructed in 1979 and is one of the most beautiful in the world. And it is really magnificent when you are swinging 160 feet above the ground in a romantic gondola and you let your gaze wander over the most beautiful city in the world. Sometimes, when it's very clear, you can even see the Alps. Is there any better place for a marriage proposal?

The **swing carousel** also goes up high in the air. The seats hang on four chains that are attached above to the carousel, and the only thing keeping you safely inside is a harness over your abdomen. The swing carousel is almost 100 years old and is fun for all ages. Flying through the air gives you a tingling feeling and you get a good view.

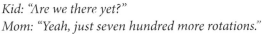

Kid: "Are we there yet?"
Mom: "Yeah, just seven hundred more rotations."

Aside from the classic swing carousel, there are crazier versions like Alexander Goetzke's "Star Flyer," where twenty-four double seats are hung on a double rotating star that swings the passengers out horizontally at 160 feet up above the Wiesn.

Those who would rather stay on the ground can let off steam at the **High Striker**. This game has been a carnival attraction for centuries. You take a heavy hammer, lift it up, and swing it down on a target. That propels a weight up a vertical tower. The stronger you hit it, the louder the applause and the more impressed your date will be. If you manage to get it all the way up to the top, a bell will ring and you will win a plastic rose. Weak little guys, made brave by beer, often try and have little success. Sometimes there are surprises, like dainty little women or frail-looking men who ring the bell. The different levels of success indicated on the tower are always funny. There's "wimp," "girly," "beginner," "rogue," and finally "ladykiller," or the highest level, where the bell rings: "world champion."

The perfect souvenir of your Oktoberfest visit is a professional **photograph**. At the end of the nineteenth century,

It's a hit!

when photography was a worldwide sensation, there were as many photographers as there were ball-throwing booths at Oktoberfest. These days there are fewer, but they are just as sought-after. You can either do a Gaudifoto, a fun photo with a silly theme and funny outfits or a nostalgia photo in costumes from the olden days. You can also have your picture taken in the tent. In 1978 Lugwig Deyl opened his photography wagon, "Zum Hoffotographen," at Oktoberfest. He collected quite an assortment of historical costumes from various theaters and flea markets, and even had some robes and dresses made by the tailor. Since 1990 the Hoffotograf has been run by Stephan Bastian. He uses the newest photography techniques and works with two professional photographers. Because he's very much in demand, you should try to get to your appointment on time.

You can of course capture your own memories with your own camera. Or with a rifle. There's been photo-shooting since 1950. You shoot at a target with an air rifle and if you get enough points, you get an instant photo as a prize.

There are all kinds of **shooting booths**. You need to have a steady hand and a well-trained eye. Then you can shoot a screwdriver, stuffed animal, or a flower for your lover. The common target of a plastic flower or screwdriver was established in 1930. Back then, players shot at clay

Every shot's a bulls eye!

pipes, while today it's usually white plastic sticks or circles. But you can still shoot at clay: in the "Altbayrischen Scherbenschießen" you aim—like the olden days—at clay pipes and targets.

For a while, a good time for the whole family has been the "Goldene Westen," where the guns are connected electronically to puppets. You stand in front of this beautiful Western scenery and you don't know where your shots are going to go. When I was young I loved shooting at Gogo the squawking vulture, the croaking fog, and the saloon pianist. You can't shoot any prizes here, but you can shoot the groundhogs, curly pig tails, or whistling

---

Recommandeur

Recommandeur is the German word for barker—the person who works at a carnival ride or booth trying to get you to play. They're holding the microphone, so they call the shots.

---

cans and see how they move and the noise they make—it's actually a lot of fun!

There are various **children's carousels** for the little ones with colorful figures, police cars, and motorcycles. When I was a kid, one of the carousels had a Popeye seat that I loved. One time, my dear parents bought me a ticket to ride but I couldn't get the prized Popeye seat because another kid was already sitting there, and I made a huge fuss. I did come to my senses, if I remember correctly, and I got a second ticket to avoid causing me any carousel trauma.

For girls, **pony rides** are always a hit—even among city girls who are typically uneasy on horseback.

The point of **bumper cars** is to ram into the others as often and as brutally as possible. You can really work up a sweat, and you need a healthy spine and good nerves. And practice. The cars have peculiar steering. If you turn the wheel too far to the right or left, the car suddenly starts driving backwards. And bam! Someone's got you in the side. And the nice smile from the guy that just hit you doesn't help. Oh, wait, I think I was the guy!

The **roller coaster** is fast and wild. There are many, some with loops, some with extra steep beginnings, some at breathtaking speeds. If you have strong nerves and strong ears, you may have fun here. You need it because female riders often give in to high-pitched shrieking—particularly on the descent. And the barker shouts in the microphone: "Going down!"

One of the classics is the Olympia Looping. It's called that because it has five rings like the Olympic logo, which the cars go around at breakneck speed.

Another good ride is the "Rund um den Tegernsee." It goes in circles and waves at an immense speed. In the 1960s, current owner's father got the idea while he was on a summer vacation at the Tegernsee lake. The idea quickly became real. There are fun little details; the cars go through a lake and under a waterfall. A water witch sprays the guest with water. When she decides to.

Getting Wet

You can get sprayed with water in the beer tent and in lots of other places at Oktoberfest. There are no limits to your fantasies. There are also rides where you can pay for this fun. For example, on the Wild Water ride or "Rund um den Tegernsee." On the latter, you have to watch out for the old witch puppet in the middle—she spits out water suddenly. On the "Top Spin," it slowly but surely  turns while you hang upside down in this monstrosity of a ride that resembles an upside-down pink sofa. You get wet. Unless you're sitting all the way in the back on the side. Then you might get lucky.

The biggest portable **wild water ride** in the world is the "Wildwasserbahn Löwenthal." It's more than 90 feet tall, splashes right into the water, and reaches a speed of more than 30 mph. Explosions and rockfalls are skillfully simulated, you rush through waterfalls, drive backward into a cave and get splashed from all directions. It's a little bit like a whitewater rafting trip. At any rate, it's amusing.

My dear friend, the Wildbach mountain guide Toni, had a great time on it. The Wildwasserbahn Löwenthal is at Oktoberfest every other year, it trades off with the Meyer-Steiger wild water ride, which is just as exciting and damp. My tip: the ride is twice as fun in nice weather, but you shouldn't sit all the way in the front, unless you want to be the wettest.

If you would rather have a drier, creepier thrill, the **haunted house** might be the thing for you. There are live ghosts, ghosts made of wood, ghosts made of cardboard, and ghosts made of metal. The experience of fantasy at the haunted house is worth a visit. It's not just about gruesomeness, it's also about handcrafted art. Haunted houses are a temple of ingenuity combined with primal fears, eroticism, and bloodthirstiness. It's good, spooky fun.

At Oktoberfest you will find the "mother of haunted houses": the "Nostalgie-Geisterbahn," owned by the old Munich performer family Eckl since 1968. I can remember the Frankenstein's monster from my earliest childhood.

In the "Shocker," you're greeted by Freddy Kruger, whose giant head reaches toward you from the façade. Inside, shadowy figures lie in wait and appear unexpectedly in the light for a few seconds, make creepy sounds, exude a musty smelling fog, and terrorize passengers passing through in the car.

The "Geisterburg" has been around since 1947. Here, the ghosts haunt on two levels. There have also been

"living" ghost sightings, and only here is the popular McMurphy, the first figure who could communicate with the audience. For a few years now, McMurphy has resided in a cage (for the safety of the audience as well as McMurphy). In front of the gate of the "Geisterschloss" the watchers are surprised by a rubber spider. That creates quite a commotion, especially among female visitors.

If you've had enough of the creeps or you need some exercise, you can do some physical work at Oktoberfest. The **swing boat** is the only ride where the motion, speed, and swing is caused by the riders themselves. At the end of the nineteenth century, swing boats for two passengers first appeared. Precursors already existed at various carnivals, for example in the Viennese amusement park Prater.

Some swing boats offer the so-called "rollover," where the ship rolls over its axis all the way, like clockwork. It takes a lot of strength and stamina, but it's worth it: a rollover is a great feast for the senses.

Some fun and affordable entertainment is the traditional **Taumler (Round Up)**. You need to use your muscles a bit here, too. You sit on the edge of a round platform and hold onto a gate. When the ride spins, you're pressed

Thrillseekers

outward and have to try not to fall over. Ladies in short dirndls have to be particularly careful that the people standing around don't see anything. And sometimes they make a flirty show of holding down their short dirndls to protect the innocent eyes of bystanders. Or not.

Centrifugal force is part of another ride, the "Rotor." The riders lean against the wall, which begins to spin. Suddenly the floor falls away from under their feet. Because of the centrifugal force, they don't fall, but rather remain stuck on the wall like flies. A fun and fascinating experience, and not just for physics students—anatomy students may also find this ride to be an interesting study.

At the **wall riders**, you get a fast-paced show. The daredevil bikers ride fearlessly on old Motorcycles straight up vertical walls, sometimes two at once. Some even manage to drive three motorcycles at once. In Pitt's Death Wall, they do world-class, breathtaking motorcycle acrobatics on a wonderful old "Indian" motorcycle from the 1920s in an oversized keg. Thrilling. Really!

The **flea circus** is also an old carnival act. In the past, it was mostly at traveling circuses. Aside from the **Kaschperl Theater**, my favorite place to be as a child was watching the performances of the talented little guys. Just a few people crowd into a small room for each performance to watch the fleas in chariot races, soccer games, or playing ball. Only feeding time is kept hidden from the public—the circus director's underarm is usually on the menu. The fleas seem to like it, since they pull their wagons with lots of strength and perseverance.

No Oktoberfest visit is complete without a stop at the **lottery**. You can buy lottery tickets for a good cause and win great things. This charitable attraction began in 1816. Then it came out that the royal family was buying a huge amount of tickets to help the poor with the money and to distribute the tickets to the needy so they could enjoy a small prize. It's obvious that such a nice tradition shouldn't end.

One of the old Oktoberfest attractions is definitely the **maze**. At the beginning of the twentieth century, the first "transparent labyrinth" was built with glass and mirror technology. The people lost in the maze always believed they knew the way, and ran into glass walls or nothingness over and over. This is an especially good time when you are slightly intoxicated. You can see confused fathers scurrying through the glass labyrinth—and just a few feet away stand their kids with tears in their eyes, unable to find their way. A tip: when you just can't go on, just look at the ground. As a rule, you can follow the footprints of other people so that you don't keep running into clear glass walls. In an emergency, the staff can also help. In front of one of the glass labyrinths there's a funny little guy in a clown costume who shakes with laughter all day. Many children don't trust him at all. I like him.

Things That Can Only Be Found at Oktoberfest

Everyone loves **Vogel-Jakob**. In 1928 a young man stood in a small show booth for the first time, and he could apparently imitate all kinds of bird sounds with his mouth. His name was Lorenz Tresenreiter and his secret was the nightingale flute developed by Professor Felix Schlimper, who was happy to give the manufacturing license to Tresenreiter. It was an ingenious idea. The size of the pipe was suitable for travel, hardly bigger than a thumbnail and called "the smallest instrument in the world," and it could make a heavenly chirp. Plus, with just a little whistle on the tongue, one person could entertain the audience all night. Vogel-Jakob is still an institution at Oktoberfest, and it's always worth watching the descendents of Lorenz Tresenreiter with their funny, fresh quips. But parents should consider what they want to get for their children. The whistle won't last forever, but long enough to have a lasting effect on the nerves.

Fogel-Jakob

In Bavaria, almost all words that begin with a "V" are pronounced as if it were an "F." There are of course exceptions, such as "vase," which would be confused with "phase" and could lead to terrible misunderstandings. (For example: "Yesterday, my wife smashed my phase.") Vitamins are "fitamins" because they keep you fit, and the Viktualienmarkt in Munich is the "Fiktualienmarkt." If that reminds you of another German word you might know, well, that's all in your head. And above all: the next person who pronounces it "Karl Valentin" has it coming!

He puts a good face on the matter.

At every performance of **Schichtl's variety show**, a person is "beheaded" by guillotine in front of the audience. Before the beheading, the audience gets a nostalgia show with dancing and a funny bit involving audience participation. It's also worth seeing the presentation in front of the tent where the Schichtl performers are presented in all their glory. There's the fat lady, the executioner (Ringo the Terrible), the executioner's assistant, Mrs. Schichtl, and the director in the form of Manfred Schauer, who has run this attraction for many years. The little food tent

Folk Singers, Speakers, and Conversationalists
Conversation is an ancient tradition in Bavaria, and much beloved. There are still many conversationalists today. You just have to know where to find them. At Oktoberfest, for example. Aside from the chatters in the beer gardens and tents, there are also professional talkers like Vogel-Jakob, Schichtl, the fresh solo performer at the Devil's Wheel, or the announcer in the Theresienwiese U-Bahn stop.

is also great. You can have a homey and atmospheric good time totally separate from the Schichtl show. Schichtl is a great old Oktoberfest tradition!

Then there's the **Revue of Illusions**. Gaby Reutlinger's stage presents the classic old illusions from traveling carnivals: "The Woman Without a Body," "The Woman Without a Head," "The Levitating Maiden," and "The Talking Head" baffle the audience just like in the old days. This illusion theater is the last of its kind in Europe. The owner is always trying to discover more traditional illusions and uphold the tradition of this carnival entertainment.

The best entertainers at Okto-berfest are the announcers at the **Devil's Wheel**. The make their living from brave and talented volunteers who try to stay on a spinning platform for as long as possible. Some people manage to do it for an

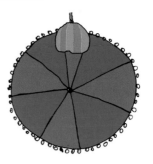

impressively long time. When it gets too crowded (or too boring) for the announcer, they use foam balls or ropes to knock even the most skilled volunteers off the Devil's Wheel. The announcer tends to hit below the belt on the riders who are holding on with all their strength. But that's part of what makes it fun. If a pretty young woman's skirt happens to ride up while she's more concerned with stay-ing on the wheel, the announcer may try to distract her with "Well, at least you shaved your legs" or "Oh, oh, that's a great outfit: a red dirndl with a white apron and yellow

Is the Earth flat after all?

Don't poke the bear!

underwear!" A young man with a less than impressive head of hair might hear "Ah, I've gone blind from the light reflecting off that head," and a retiree "Be careful you don't lose your dentures!" Something unique about this attraction is that you pay an entry fee, sit down (to enjoy the Schadenfreude, or pleasure derived from the misfortunes of others, you get from the announcer's comments while the people try their hardest on the wheel), and you can stay as long as you want. Even hours if you want. They aren't wasted hours. The Devil's Wheel is my personal favorite attraction at Oktoberfest. Karl Valentin, the famous Bavarian comedian from the early 1900s, loved it, too.

Just a few examples of the **Mystic Swing** can still be found at carnivals. There's one at Oktoberfest. You go through a small door into a beautifully decorated room with a swing in the middle that seats 20 people and is attached to a shaft. It swing back and forth faster and faster, until you're suddenly upside down. After awhile, you realize that the room is actually moving and it's all a well staged illusion.

The "turning house" is an old carnival attraction where the room is spun around you from the outside, creating the impression that you're the one spinning, and not the room. The sense of weightlessness is just an illusion. The Mystic Swing is completely safe, with no need for seat belts or harnesses. Lots of fun!

Though it might sound like it, the **Krinoline** isn't a puffy petticoat with hoops many of wood, whalebone, or steel, but rather one of the oldest carnival rides in Munich. The rolling platform is reminiscent of a fine lady's crinoline from those days. It tumbles around and up

Guests have been spinning here nonstop since 1924.

and down. The riders sit right near the band. Yes, the Krinoline has its own band! Lots of guests know the repertoire and make requests that are cheerfully filled. The guests give tips just as cheerfully. Everyone's happy.

On the Krinoline, the operators play host first, wait until it's going, then jump on and collect the money. That's how it was 88 years ago, when the jubilee Krinoline ran for the first time, and that's how it is today. It really gets going, so let it take you for a ride. The Krinoline is faster than it looks.

The **Russian Wheel** is the small form of the Ferris wheel. Josef Esterl, the grandfather of the current owner, put his new ride into action in July of 1925. It originally had a carved facade with paintings that were exchanged for the current ones in the 1950s. Until about 1960 it was the biggest Ferris wheel in southern Germany, with 12 gondolas a height of 45 feet.

The fun starts on the **Toboggan** when you start climbing up: riders have to try to keep their balance on the conveyor belt that carries them up. The conveyor belt pulls you along quickly and not everyone manages to stay upright. People

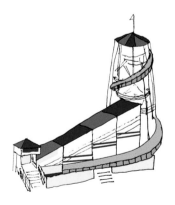

Stand on your own two feet.

who are a little tipsy have it really hard. But the greatest entertainment for the watchers gathered by the old wooden tower are drunken men who lose their footing in their Haferl shoes and are carried up on the conveyor belt kicking like beetles on their backs. Schadenfreude is rarely so cheerful and guilt-free. After the little ride on the conveyor belt, there are some stairs to go up on foot. At the end, you sit on a little square rug and zoom back down the big, curved wooden slide. Everyone manages the sliding with ease.

The multi-track "**Münchner Rutschn**" is the second-oldest slide ride at Oktoberfest, after the Toboggan. You climb up to the top on foot like you're climbing a mountain. Then you get a little rug square and you whiz down the wide, blue and white mogul slope. It's really very fun. It's also fun to race your friends. If you get the chance, glance at the elaborate paintings on the trailer: an artist has immortalized fabulous Oktoberfest scenes.

My tip: if you've drunk a bit too much and you're feeling sick of beer, just go for a slide and you'll have the courage and strength for another stein.

The **Zugspitzbahn** (mountain train) is also lively. It's over 50 years old but it's fast and fun. It can keep up with most of the other rides.

If you stick to the rules, the mountain is your friend.

It's decorated as a white and blue winter wonderland complete with snowmen and snow-frosted evergreen trees. The two-seater gondolas race through the charming winter landscape with lots of tossing and swinging—and they do it in later summer. Then it really takes off. Sssssssst.

Tip: thanks to centrifugal force, the person sitting on the inside is always pushed against the strong shoulder of the person sitting on the outside. So, my dear men, sit on the outside if you don't want to squash your date.

Historical Oktoberfest

For the 200th anniversary of Oktoberfest in 2010, there was a family-friendly, much more peaceful and nostalgic "extra fest" in the southern part of the Theresienwiese: the "Oide Wiesn" or Historical Oktoberfest.

In addition to many historical show booths and carousels, there were two big festival tents, one of which offered an old Bavarian-style atmosphere, and the other which showed culture and customs. They avoided colorful modern decorations. Instead, they hung evergreen garlands and created a traditional Bavarian festival tent atmosphere.

There was also an anniversary beer just for the Historical Oktoberfest jointly created by the six traditional Munich breweries: Augustiner, Hacker-Pschorr, Hofbräu, Löwenbräu, Paulaner, and Spatenbräu. This special beer was amber colored and had a full-bodied malt taste.

Cozy gondolas.

It was pulled from big wooden kegs and served in stone mugs like it was 200 years ago. The menu in the historical tent offered traditional Munich dishes like Rumford's soup and Munich-style weisswurst.

There were also horse races, a museum tent with Schuhplattlers and Goaßlschnalzers and countless other attractions that were very well received by the public. There was also an animal tent where various domestic animals and livestock could be seen.

The prices were also from the olden days. The Historical Oktoberfest did have an entry fee, but only 4 euros. All the offerings like the performances in the culture tent and the horse races were included in the price. Just carousel rides and show booths were an extra euro. The Bavarian actor and radio icon Conny Glogger was moved to tears when she discovered her favorite childhood carousel ride at the Historical Oktoberfest.

The Historical Oktoberfest was only supposed to be set up for the 200th anniversary of Oktoberfest, but it was so popular that it happened again in 2011. Because of the central agricultural festival that happens every four years in the southern part of the Theresienwiese, it didn't appear again in 2012. The Munich city council is debating whether to offer the Historical Oktoberfest to nostalgic fans as a regular event alongside the big Oktoberfest.

Around Oktoberfest

The After-Oktoberfest Parties

For party people who just can't get enough, there are plenty of of establishments that offer you the option of further partying. Before you start a pointless debate with the tent security, it's better to keep your good mood and move on to the next party. But watch out: Oktoberfest goers are not welcomed everywhere with open arms. There are places with signs posted reading, "No Tracht Allowed" ("Hier nicht mit Tracht"). It might seem strange to outsiders, but Oktoberfest is an exception for Munich natives. We don't run around in lederhosen all year. Just most of the time.

A really great option for continuing your Oktoberfest evening is **Substanz** at Ruppertstraße 28. There's good rock music, good beer, good schnapps, and a real Bavarian bar atmosphere. Plus, you're welcome to come in Tracht. It's about a 10-minute walk from the Bavaria statue to Substanz.

The **Alte Kongresshalle** is equally easy to find. It's directly behind the Bavaria statue and is reachable in just a few minutes by foot, even in a very drunken state. It's a club, but the mood goes well with Oktoberfest. Here you can let loose until the wee hours of the morning.

The third place that's right next to the Wiesn is the **Wiesnclub** in the Hacker-Pschorr-Bräuhaus. Wiesn Hits, cheerful people, and a fun mood prevail all night. The doors open at 9:00 p.m. and you should do your best to show up before the bar closes at Oktoberfest unless you want to wait in line forever. The same is true of all the after-Oktoberfest party spots.

The **After-Wiesn-Zelt** in Stiglmaierplatz (right next to the Löwenbräukeller) offers a beer tent atmosphere. It's a good 20-minute walk from the main entrance of Oktoberfest, and correspondingly longer depending on drunkenness level. However, it's worth the visit.

I do not recommend the rather low-class dive bars (mostly pretty run-down) around the main train station. There's often a terrible atmosphere and your fun evening can have a really dismal end. In and of itself, I'm not opposed to visiting dive bars, but after Oktoberfest the tragic quiet, the tragic guests, and their tragic stories can be just too depressing.

A great place to spend the rest of an Oktoberfest night is the **Fraunhofer Schoppenstube** at Fraunhoferstraße 41—that's right next to the Fraunhoferstraße U-Bahn station and can be reached easily by taking the U-Bahn one station from Theresienwiese to the Hauptbahnhof, transferring to the U1 or U2 and going two more stops. In the Fraunhofer Schoppenstube you'll find real old Munich friendliness embodied by the charming host, Gerti. Her wine recommendations are always perfect for the guests' tastes and her meatballs are some of the best I've ever had. You can party here until the morning, singing and laughing, so everyone should be sure to pay a visit to this excellent establishment. Just like the rest of the year, the night isn't just for sleeping!

The **Zephyr**, a classic cocktail bar with a relaxed and cheerful atmosphere, is just a minute from the Fraunhofer Schoppenstube at Baaderstraße 68. The well-trained staff prepare high-quality drinks with fresh fruit and first-class spirits. You get to the Zephyr the exact same way from Oktoberfest as to the Fraunhofer Schoppenstube (or at least it's also near the Fraunhoferstraße U-Bahn station).

You would be well advised to head to the bar **Zum Wolf** at Pestalozzistraße 68. You can reach it by foot in a good 10 to 15 minutes from the Oktoberfest exit on Mozartstraße. From Mozartstraße, go left on Lindwurmstraße to Reisingerstraße, then left onto Thalkirchner Straße for a few feet, then a quick right into Stephansplatz— and there you are on Pestalozzistraße, with the bar on the right-hand side. When you've found the bar, the finest cocktails, fresh beer, and casual sound make a brilliant impression. Balu provides the fabulous drinks and Wolfi provides the fabulous music. This is recommended for a nice nightcap after an Oktoberfest visit.

Jan and Filip, the managers of **Valentinstüberl** at Dreimühlenstraße 28, are always in a great mood, eloquent, and ready for almost any scandal. The guests at this establishment are just as colorful and cheerful. It's one of the coolest spots in Munich, with Czech beer, excellent spirits, radio plays on the bathroom speakers, and a very relaxed party atmosphere. The Valentinstüberl can easily be reached from the south side of the Wiesn with the 152 bus (Hans-Fischer-Straße stop, toward the Ostbahnhof). Get off at the Ehrengutstraße stop. It's just a few steps from there.

In Johannisplatz, not far from the Max-Weber-Platz U-Bahn stop, is the cult establishment called **Johanniscafe**. The pearl of Haidhausen! The host is named Olaf and each night he personally sees to the physical and mental well-being of his guests, who are always satisfied and happy. Night owls can continue their lively and exuberant partying here until well into the morning. And the best part: you just get on the train at Theresienwiese and off at Max-Weber-Platz, since the U4 (toward Arabellapark) and the U5 (toward Neuperlach Süd) connect these two stations. Excellent.

There are more good after-Oktoberfest parties in P1, in the Parkcafé, in the Milchbar, in 8 Below, in the 089-Bar, in Lenbach, in Max und Moritz or right in the Kultfabrik. There's something for every taste.

The Oktoberfest Museum

A few steps from the Isartor, somewhat hidden at Sterneckerstraße 2, you will find the Beer and Oktoberfest Museum. There are little stairways, nooks, and hallways and lots of lovely things to see, such at old Oktoberfest postcards collected by Oktoberfest celebrity Willy Heide (1919–2011). There are also many other lovingly arranged little Oktoberfest details, starting with the tokens that Ludwig I of Bavaria and his Therese threw to the cheering crowd from their carriage on their wedding day and the first day of Oktoberfest. They have the wonderful name "Wedding Tokens," and it makes quite

the impression when you consider that the two famous spouses held those tokens in their own hands. You can rummage through various drawers where you can find rare pieces of past exhibitions.

Then there's the iron crown of hops that hung over inns to show that beer was served there. You will learn a lot about beer, about the guild stars of the breweries, and that there were once over 60 breweries in Munich. Just imagine that kind of confusion at today's Oktoberfest! The only brewery that is still family-owned is Augustiner-Bräu.

From the highest floor right under the roof, a steep staircase called the "ladder to heaven" leads right to the street, which was common in many Munich houses a hundred years ago. The building that houses the Beer and Oktoberfest Museum was build in 1327 after the big fire (about the same time as the Isartor, which was a part of the city wall then). Luckily, it could be restored to its original form.

The Oktoberfest Museum contains one more thing: an ancient, old Bavarian taproom and other old bars, displayed on separate levels and connected by little stairs, all very enchanting and Munich-esque! A toast to the

Munich Beer and Oktoberfest Museum and its friendly and helpful curator, Lukas Bulka!

The best way to reach the Oktoberfest Museum is by foot from Marienplatz.

The Puppet Theater and Entertainment Section of the Munich Stadtsmuseum

This is a part of the museum's permanent collection and can be seen year round. I highly recommend it. The focus was originally on puppet theater, but since 1980 the museum has been expanding its interests to include entertainment, particularly attractions at German carnivals and fairs from the nineteenth century to the present. Vaudeville and the circus are also included. And of course, there are highlights from Oktoberfest. The cultural scholar and acting director of the Stadtmuseum, Florian Dering, organized this area with much care. There are many worthwhile things to see here, for example a complete horror panopticon, the old King Kong of a nostalgic haunted house, a curious shooting game with a scared dictator putting up his hands, a head behind bars that suddenly begins screaming and spitting blood, and other lovely, gruesome, and nostalgic cultural items. The Stadtmuseum is also just a short walk from Marienplatz.

Final Tips

- Servers are very important; everything depends on them. So, be nice to them and give them tips.
- Please refrain from offering tips to police officers.
- In the event of mass panic, save the clothespins with your server's or friend's name on them.
- Always be punctual, because having to wait at Oktoberfest is no fun. Every second counts. (Otherwise: tent closed, girlfriend gone, beer flat.)
- In your bag, you should always have: ID, money, and a key (to get back home).
- What you should leave home: wallet with credit cards and other important things.
- Don't drink so much that you end up doing things you'll regret.
- Answer the call of nature only in the designated areas.
- Not all of Oktoberfest is good for a family outing. Children under sixteen may not be on the fairgrounds after 8:00 p.m. without an adult escort. Children under six may only be in beer tents with an adult until 8:00 p.m. Strollers are only allowed from Sunday to Friday until 6:00 p.m. On Saturdays, strollers are generally prohibited.

- Animals must stay home. Service dogs are the exception, of course.
- Alcoholic drinks are available on the fairgrounds; bringing alcohol from home is not allowed.
- Dangerous items like pepper spray, guns, knives, etc. do not belong at Oktoberfest.

Reservations

You should plan your Oktoberfest visit very far in advance since many people (rightfully) want to visit and there is a limited number of seats. In every tent there are seats that can't be reserved, so if you can't get a reservation, you should just get there early—in my over 30 years of Oktoberfest experience, I've never heard of anyone who couldn't get a seat or a beer at all. In a pinch, you just have to  be patient and it will work out. There are also always the beer gardens, where no seats can be reserved. I, myself, have often sat outside with a few excellent servers, sometimes even in pouring rain. The beer tastes just as good, and there's great cheer to be had outside, too.

But it is still a good idea to start planning for a specific Oktoberfest at the beginning of the year. You can find endless information on the internet about how and when to reserve; if you put in a little effort, you'll surely get a seat in a box, in the center, or in the gallery. There are two reservation times, either afternoon or evening. Daytime reservations generally begin at 11:00 a.m. or noon and end at the beginning of the evening shift, which goes from 5:00 to 10:30 p.m. Most tents close at 11:00 p.m., so the latest you can get a beer is at 10:30. A few tents stay open longer, and they have different reservation times. Unfortunately, a new method has started to creep in, where afternoon tables are reserved in two-hour blocks. That's disgusting, and those hosts should be ashamed, because that's only enough time to get a baseline buzz, not to have a real Oktoberfest celebration.

The standard reservation is a "normal" beer table that fits 10 people. There is often a minimum of two beers and a half roast chicken per person, which can be paid in advance in exchange for coupons. The beer tents with "normal" hours tend to stick to this "normal" require-ment. If you want to be different and go to the tents that are open later, you will probably have to dig a little deeper in your pocket.

Some enterprising people try to make some money by buy-ing up reservations and selling them privately for a markup. This is shameful and rotten and shouldn't be supported.

For example: a loving wife plans to celebrate her hus-band's birthday in a beer tent and she reserves a table for

10 in January. Then she realizes that her spouse's sister is planning a celebration at Lake Starnberg at the same time, and the Oktoberfest visit falls through. The wife is now sitting on 10 chicken coupons and 20 beer coupons, which cost over 285 euros. If  she decides to sell the whole reservation to her coworker for 300 euros, it's legitimate, and no one would comment. But there are other situations. For example, a friend of mine from Hesse won a reservation for 320 euros on an internet auction in a tent that I particularly love and often frequent. He quickly sent the money and then the envelope with the reservation ticket arrived. But the coupons were missing. He looked up the auction page and realized that it simply said "reservation from 5:00 p.m. to 10:30 p.m. in the center area." There was nothing in the description about coupons, so there was nothing he could legally do. Outside Germany in 2011, many counterfeit reservations were sold for horrendous prices and the poor tourists from Korea, Italy, Australia, or Cameroon got into fights with the tent hosts over the documents instead of a friendly Oktoberfest visit. So this is my emphatic advice: Reserve early and through the normal channels! I've included a sample e-mail to help you.

Reservation Request Example

Subject: Reservation for (your full name)

I would like to reserve a table for 10 in (tent). Possible times:

 (list several options of days)

 Time: after 17:00

 My Name:

 (Name)

 (Address)

Please schedule my reservation for one of these days. If there is no availability on the listed days, please suggest an alternative time.

Best Wishes,

(Name)

Afterword: Bavarian Tradition

People say that tradition isn't preserving the ashes, it's keeping the fire burning. Sometimes you'll hear northern Germans at Oktoberfest say, "It's just a big drunken party. It doesn't have anything to do with tradition anymore." But it does. Because Bavarian tradition includes beer drinking and feasting and drinking songs and Tracht and markets and Trachten clubs and fairs and grumpiness and Charivari and gentianflowers and nonsense

Hold on tightly to the present. Every situation, every moment is of infinite worth, for it is the representative of a whole eternity.
Johann Wolfgang von Goethe (1749–1832)

and knee socks and saucy dirndls and dashing young men and fresh quips and Kini Ludwig and stubbornness and regionalism and Alpine humor and Alpine charm and winter sports and beer gardens and the Kocherlballand country life and country air and butchers and brewers and the German Beer Purity Law and craziness and agitators and revolutionaries and folk singers and conversationalists and pubs and newcomers and summer visitors and natives and almost-natives and innate skepticism and innate thirst and innate extravagance and chivalry and family and coziness and friendliness and wantonness and piousness and the blue sky and mountain winds and devotion to Mary and maypoles. Got it?

Personality Test for Oktoberfest Goers

Am I really ready for Oktoberfest? Do I have the right character to completely enjoy the greatest folk festival in the world? What sort of personality do I really have?

Answer the following eleven questions honestly and straightforwardly. The results will amaze you!

1. You've been looking forward to eating a pork knuckle all day. Shortly after ordering, the restaurant tells you that there aren't any more. What do you do?
a) I say, "I have a reservation. I insist on receiving my order."
b) I look for something else on the menu.
c) I ask the server to recommend something else.

2. You buy yourself a T-shirt. What sort of design do you choose?
a) Solid color.
b) Che Guevara.
c) "Beer helps me keep this figure."

3. You're the passenger in a friend's car. You take a break at a rest stop. What do you buy as provisions?

a) A pre-packaged triangular sandwich and a multi-vitamin drink.
b) An apple and a coffee to go.
c) Two beers and a deli sandwich with pickles.

4. You're planning your next summer vacation. Which is the closest to your vacation choice?
a) Greece.
b) The Jersey Shore.
c) Mallorca.

5. What do you dress up as on Karnival or Halloween?
a) I don't dress up. It's nonsense.
b) Cowboy, Indian, or Pirate.
c) The most stupid and absurd thing I can think of.

6. Your 15-year-old daughter comes home late at night, apparently drunk. How do you react?
a) I say, "You'll definitely regret that in the morning!"
b) I say, "Well done! If you just get tipsy, you're throwing money away!"
c) I ground her, obviously.

7. What would you do if you won a million dollars in the Lotto?
a) Finally renovate the house.

b) Save it for a rainy day.

c) Invite my friends on a world tour and paint the town red.

8. Happy hour ends in 10 minutes. What do you do?

a) I quickly order two more cocktails.

b) I get the check. I'm not going to pay full price for drinks.

c) I ask my friends if they want to stay, and then I decide.

9. You're at the beer garden. All the tables are partly in use, but there are still some individual seats. What do you do?

a) I wait until there's a free table. If it takes too long, I'll go somewhere else.

b) I ask the servers if they can help me.

c) I go to a table with friendly-looking people and ask if I can sit with them.

10. You're on a public bus that has just stopped at the bus stop. You see a man running, but he obviously won't catch it. What do you do?

a) I think, "Well, let's see if he makes it."

b) I stand in the door and hold it open until the man has reached the bus.

c) I probably wouldn't even notice.

Points:

	A	B	C
1	0	2	1
2	2	1	0
3	0	1	2
4	2	1	0
5	0	1	2
6	1	2	0
7	0	1	2
8	2	0	1
9	1	0	2
10	1	2	0

Scoring:

0–8 Points

You seem a bit too reserved for Oktoberfest. Face your fears! Be jolly and carefree. Life is too beautiful to drive around with the parking brake on all the time.

9–14 Points

You're a sociable person, but maybe sometimes a bit too opportunistic. When you're choosing your beer tent, you should probably choose a traditional one. After you've had a glass or two, you can move to a wilder tent. But keep yourself a bit reserved and observe the colorful activity. Keep your life story to yourself. Have fun!

15–18 Points

You're definitely on the right track. All you need is two or three test visits, and it'll be perfect.

19–22 Points

You are a smooth customer and a perfect Oktoberfest visitor. You can do what you want; you don't need a role model. Carry on!

Thanks to:

Andrea
Barbara
Benedikt
Bianca
Conny Glogger
Coxies along with Didi
Franz
Franzilein
Hansi Krohn
Hegi
Julchen
Kerstin
Lukas Bulka
Marckus and his family
Maus
Meikelchen
Micha

Peter Eichhorn and his
　team
Raben
Richie Westermaier
Rico Grabowski
Sandilein
Silvia
Stefan
Steffilein
Stevie
Sudelmann
Tanthe
Tobi Haberstroh
Tom
Tuscher
Vroni von Quast
Wöbbel